THE PENT[LAND HILLS]
By WILLIAM ANDERSON
('W. A.')

LONDON: 38 Soho Square, W.1

W. & R. CHAMBERS, LIMITED
EDINBURGH: 339 High Street

1926

TO MY COMRADES

WHO, BY THEIR COMPANIONSHIP,

BY FIT SPEECH AND BY FIT SILENCE,

HAVE ADDED TO THE ENJOYMENT OF MANY

A PENTLAND WALK.

Printed in Great Britain.
W. & R. CHAMBERS, LTD., LONDON and EDINBURGH.

PREFACE.

I MAKE no apology for coming before the public with another book on the Pentland Hills, because I do not propose to treat the subject on the same lines as those already published. This is not a guide-book; it is rather an appreciation of the Pentland Hills by an ardent lover of them.

It is well over forty years since I made my first acquaintance with the Pentlands, and during the greater part of that time I have been one of their most regular visitants. I adopt, and apply to the hills, the words which Ruskin uses regarding mountains: 'To me they are the beginning and the end of all natural scenery.' Of recent years my feeling towards the hills has been somewhat of the nature of a passion. It is as if all the memories of early years spent in a hilly district were coming back in a full flood-tide, which is carrying me resistlessly with it. The call of the hills is most commanding, and it must be obeyed. In truth, there is no thought of disobeying it. Let the weather be what it may; let the wind be never so high or cold; be it warm sunshine or biting frost, rain, hail, or snow, the knapsack is shouldered, the stick is seized, and the call is joyfully obeyed.

I put away from me the thought that the time is fast approaching when I must give up going to the hills. I go there to keep that spectre from getting to close grips, to keep it at arm's length, and I feel that the action serves the purpose excellently. I commend it to the young, to the middle-aged, and to those who, like myself, though advanced in years, are striving to keep youthful in spirit.

To me the compilation of this book has been a thanksgiving for many days of rare enjoyment, many nights of

consequent dreamless sleep; perfect health; sound digestion; much moral and intellectual stimulus; many friend-
ships made; fellowship with Nature—in fact, for most
things which tend to make life pleasant and profitable.
All of these have been attained by persistent tramping
over the Pentlands.

I have endeavoured to describe not only the hills, but
what I have seen *on* them—birds, beasts, and flowers;
and what I have seen *from* them—views, sunsets, sunrises,
mist and other atmospheric effects, nightfall and moonlight; believing that such things are of perennial interest
to every intelligent person.

No single thing recorded here is set down from hearsay.
The notes regarding birds, beasts, and flowers, the varied
appearances of the hills, and the atmospheric effects, are
in every case the results of personal observation. I have
measured the part of the terraqueous globe comprehended
within the area of the Pentland Hills, as Carlyle says in
Sartor Resartus, with 'a pair of compasses which belong
exclusively to myself.' Consequently, I have missed some
things which other writers have seen; and, it may be, I
have seen some things which other writers have missed.
Various birds which are said to inhabit, or visit, the hills
I have not yet had the pleasure of meeting, and sundry
flowers and plants which are said to be natives are still
strangers to me. But a hill-tramper never knows what
his luck may be. Any day one of these gay revellers may
flash across my vision, causing a catch in my breath, and
leaving a picture in my brain, which, like 'the smell of
violets hidden in the grass,' will come back to me in after
years, enriched and glorified through the purple haze of
memory's sunset air. Therefore is the hill-walker observant. He sees visions and he dreams dreams, but he walks
with the open eye and he sees things. He goes in the spirit
of adventure, and adventures do not fail to come his way.

I wish I could convey to the non-walker some idea, if only a faint one, of the pleasure and profit that follow in the train of the tramper. Such will be my endeavour now. I strive to be a recruiting sergeant, beating up recruits for the noble army of walkers; or an apostle, or evangelist preaching an old faith—faith in the virtue and efficacy of rational open-air exercise.

The Pentland Hills offer almost everything that is wanted by the seeker after health, the seeker after beauty, and the lover of Nature.

In conclusion, I have to express my thanks to the proprietors of *The Scotsman* for liberty to make use of portions of articles and Nature Notes contributed at various times to its pages, and too numerous to mention in detail. I have also to thank the many Pentland trampers who have assisted me with suggestions and encouragement in the compilation and arrangement of this little book.

A View from Allermuir Hill, looking West.

[Reading from left to right the peaks are: Castlelaw, Turnhouse Hill, Carnethy, South Black Hill, Scald Law, Gap Law, East Kip, West Kip, Green Law, The Mount, Byrehope Mount, Wether Law, Black Hill, East Cairn Hill.]

CONTENTS.

	PAGE
GENERAL FEATURES	13
LEGEND AND HISTORY	46
THE PEAKS	60
VIEWS—IN SUNSHINE AND STORM	98
FAUNA	117
FLORA	144
EPILOGUE	161

WIND OF THE HILLS.

Oh! wind of the hills! with your clear nipping breath,
   Sweeping round from the sea and the bens,
You bring light to the eye, you bring life, you bring
     death,
   As you rush over peaks and through glens.

Oh! wind of the hills! from the south softly blow,
   Though you bring with you thunder and rain;
Like the Mother Earth's voice crooning softly and low,
   You bring rest to the heart and the brain.

Oh! wind of the hills! blow cold from the north,
   Over bents with their bowed withered heads,
Though there's death in your wake as your spear launches
     forth,
   And want where your icy foot treads.

Oh! wind of the hills! blow raw from the east,
   Though laden with mist and with sleet;
Your robe is a shroud, and a famine your feast,
   And white are the paths of your feet.

Oh! wind of the hills! from the west blow loud;
   Bring the scents of the earth and the seas,
With rain slanting down from the big white cloud,
   And your sounding song in the trees.

Oh! wind of the hills! blow wherever you list,
   And bring with you whate'er you care;
Bring the frost or the rain, bring sunshine, bring mist,
   If I'm there—if only I'm there.

AT THE END OF THE JOURNEY

The Tramper to his Friend.

WHEN on my day of life the night is falling,
  And the sun sinks behind Time's purpling hills,
May no remorseful moaning wind be calling
  Of thoughtless follies done, or dull remembered ills.

But as a tired tramper may I fall asleep,
  Leaving the waking to the coming morn;
No idle dreaming head be mine, but slumber deep
  Of him who is aweary and wayworn.

And when I'm fallen asleep and all is still,
  And the tired limbs and weary heart are both at
    rest,
Shed no external tear; but, if you will,
  Shed heart tears for me in your loving breast.

THE PENTLAND HILLS.

GENERAL FEATURES.

THE Pentland Hills are situated mainly in Midlothian, but partly also in the counties of
Lanark and Peebles. They terminate, at their
north-eastern end, slightly beyond the fourth mile-
stone from Tollcross, Edinburgh, and almost due
south from the city. Thence they extend in a
south-westerly direction a distance of some sixteen
or seventeen miles, with a breadth of from four
to six miles, and an area (roughly) between eighty
and ninety square miles. At their north-eastern
extremity their slopes are steep and their outlines imposing; the rocks cropping out
in places giving them a bold appearance,
which, in certain atmospheric conditions,
approaches to grandeur and sublimity. At their
south-western extremities they terminate in wide
heathery muirs, which slope gently down into
Clydesdale.

Outlines and Structure.

At their north-eastern end the hills are dry, and,
during most of the year, pleasant to traverse. At
the other end they are wet and spongy, not only
in winter, but sometimes during a considerable
portion of the summer.

For the most part, they are softly rounded, homely-looking hills, grass- or heather-clad to their tops. There are, however, exceptions to this, which will be noticed in due course. In height they vary from about 1200 or 1300 feet to nearly 1900 feet, Scald Law, the highest peak, being 1898 feet above sea-level. All of them bear evidence of having been subjected to long and severe glacial action. The movement of the ice has been mainly from north-west to south-east in direction. Several of the boulders left stranded amongst the hills have evidently been brought from a distance, and one of them, a mica slate, said to weigh between eight and ten tons, is supposed to have travelled from Argyleshire.

It has been variously estimated by geologists that the hills were at one time from five thousand to eight thousand feet higher than at present, which gives an idea of the enormous amount of denudation they have undergone. The *kaims*, or gravel mounds, east of Hillend; in the valley of the Glencorse Burn, west from Flotterstone Bridge; and at other places, indicate where the detritus—mostly rocks, sand, and gravel borne by the glaciers—has been deposited when the ice began to melt on its approach to the sea. The sand now being taken from the pit at Comiston is believed by Mr Peach, of the Geological Survey, to have been deposited in a lake formed there by the ' melt water ' of the glaciers.

Geologists tell us that the north-eastern Pentland peaks are of volcanic origin. This, perhaps, accounts for their bolder outlines. The long, rather featureless slopes at the south-western end belong mainly to the conglomerate formation. The East and West Cairn Hills and some of the lower heights adjacent to them appear to be the only peaks of real rock formation. The rock, which is of Old Red Sandstone age, crops out at various places, and has been fantastically shaped and carved by the weather.

Attempts have been made, more than once, to group the hills into 'masses,' but, as the author of the latest attempt frankly admits, such grouping is arbitrary, and therefore serves no useful purpose. It may, however, be said that, beginning at the north-eastern end, the Pentlands run in two ranges, separated by the Loganlee glen, which follows, mainly, the general direction of the heights. The northern range, which projects about two miles more to the north-east than its neighbour, extends a distance of five miles, and includes the peaks of Caerketton, Allermuir, Capelaw, Harbour Hill, Bell's Hill, and Black Hill, all fairly well in line, with Castlelaw a little to the south. The southern range extends a distance of three miles, and includes Turnhouse Hill, Carnethy, Scald Law, and the East and West Kips, all lying more or less in line with South Black Hill a little to the south. From the termination of these two ranges the hills run to the south-west practically in one mass, intersected by various shallow valleys, which cut them mainly at right angles to their south-westerly direction. Some of these valleys cross the hills, while others run into and are lost in their sides. These transverse valleys have apparently been 'produced by streams of greater volume than those now draining them,' streams which are taking a different course than formerly, having been captured during the evolution of the land by streams running in other directions.

There are two principal valleys or glens, the Medwin and the Loganlee. The Medwin, which

Valleys and Glens.

is a continuation of the valley between the Pentlands and the Peeblesshire hills about Dolphinton, runs north some three miles into the heart of the Pentlands, and is a pretty pastoral valley. About a mile up from the cottage of Medwinhead is Roger's Kirk, a reputed meeting-place of the Covenanters, where the small stream, forgetting its usual placid, decorous behaviour, brawls a little as it tumbles over stones in its passage through the rocky gorge which hems it in. Roger's Kirk is not the ruin of an ecclesiastical building, as some have thought, and as its name might imply, but a roughly-shaped amphitheatre. Probably it derived its name from having been a meeting-place of the Covenanters, where they listened to the preaching of some one bearing the name of Roger. Higher up the valley two short lateral valleys, both of them bearing the name of Raven's Cleuch, join it from the east. Down each of them a tiny tributary of the Medwin tumbles prettily in a series of cascades. A little farther down the stream than Roger's Kirk a trickle of water comes in from the west. It has excavated a short valley, known as Fingerstane Cleuch, a picturesque spot, dotted all over with clumps of the handsome male-fern of a lovely colour, the stools of a great height bearing witness to the length of time they have flourished there. These cleuchs are delightsome places, in which one might loaf and

dream away a whole summer's day. Near the top
of the Medwin valley, on a rock beside the stream,
the names I. KER and I. PORTES (Porteous) have
been rudely cut. One wonders if the cutting dates
from Covenanting times, or if it is only an example
of modern rustic lettering, perhaps the names of a
lover and his lass. At the head of the stream
some really fine cliffs rise from the water's edge,
cliffs which would look much finer but for the fact
that the stone composing them is soft and rotten,
and all its sharpness has been worn off by the action
of the weather.

The Medwin is not, however, to be compared with
the Loganlee valley—or, perhaps, one should say
glen—out of which rise the finest hills in the whole
Pentland range; and the reservoirs of Glencorse
and Loganlee, which fill up so much of it, although
sometimes ignorantly spoken of as ponds, are quite
as fine as many of the more vaunted Highland lochs.
To tramp through this valley or glen between, say,
Flotterstone Bridge and the waterfall beyond Loganlee Reservoir, or even to continue the walk through
the Green Cleuch to Bavelaw on a fine summer
evening or on a sharp winter day, or in fact in
any suitable weather at any season of the year, is
to enjoy a rare pleasure; while by climbing one
of the hills rising out of the glen—Castlelaw, for
instance—a glorious view will be obtained. It
matters not whether the day be one of clear sunshine or of fitful shadow; the mist may be envelop-
ing the hill-tops, or trailing along their sides; the
peaks may stand out dazzlingly white, or be blurred
with rain; their broad haunches may be carpeted

with the crimson and the gold of the spring blaeberries; autumn may throw its royal mantle over
them; or winter may whiten the bents, and trans-
form the brackens into glowing orange,—in every
season, under every condition, the view up the
Loganlee glen is one of rare beauty. The evening
effects are surpassingly lovely.

There are other little green glens and valleys,
short and long, hidden away in the heart of the
hills; but one almost fears to speak of them, because
to enter any of them is to trespass. At the risk
of having this little book labelled 'A Guide for
Trespassers,' I mention one or two of them. The
first I will refer to runs almost due west from the
North Esk Reservoir, having Wether Law to the
north, and The Mount and Deerhope Rig to the
south. There is a beautiful spring of clear cool
water in it, of which one may drink and thank the
giver. The tramper may follow this valley to its
head, and then make his way to the summit of
Mount Maw, from which he may continue his ramble
in whatever direction suits his liking or his time.

A pleasant place, too, is the Threshie Dean, a
short, shallow glen, about a mile west of Listonshiels,
running up into the ample bosom of the East Cairn
Hill, with the inevitable little burn, a very tiny
one in this case, tinkling down the bottom. The
threshies (rushes) are still there, but the trees which
once covered the slopes now lie, for the most part,
like unburied dead on a battlefield, victims of old
age and rough weather. Many of them are rotted
into touchwood, which the kindly earth is absorbing
into itself.

There are also the Howden Glen—the top of which St Ives passed in company with the drovers— formerly known under the more poetical name of How Dene, between Capelaw and Allermuir Hill; Den's Cleuch, between Bell's Hill and Black Hill; the Maiden Cleuch, forming part of the path from Currie to Glencorse; the Green Cleuch, through which the Balerno path passes to Glencorse, one of

Howden Glen.

the pleasantest paths in all the Pentlands; Wether Linn, near the Cauld Stane Slap (where fossils have been found), besides other nameless, but romantic, rocky, little linns, cleuchs, and hopes, running a few score yards into the hills, and looking, some of them, as if they had been suddenly gashed out of the hill- side by a waterspout or cloudburst, as occasionally does happen in hilly districts. The Loganlee Habbie's Howe is a level stretch of greensward, through which the Logan Burn meanders pleasantly in summer, and sometimes rushes very fiercely in winter, overflowing its banks and depositing gravel far above its normal level. At the end of the howe, behind the screen of trees which bield it from the angry airt, sits the cottage of the Loganlee herd. By its cosy fireside I have often secured shelter from wintry blasts, and

The Shepherd's Cottage, Loganlee; Castlelaw in the background.

enjoyed the kindly hospitality and the racy conversation of its inmates.

Of the many little rivers and streams which rise amongst the Pentlands, all, with one exception, take more or less easterly or westerly courses, and discharge their waters into either the Firth of Forth or the Clyde. The single exception is the Lyne, which, with its tributary burns, descends towards the Borderland and joins the Tweed. Geologists are of opinion that the Lyne alone of all the Pentland streams preserves its original course.

Streams and Springs.

The presence, or otherwise, of good drinking water is a matter of great importance to hill-walkers.

The Pentlands in this respect are amply provided. There are a number of excellent springs; some of them, indeed, of superexcellence—the hotter the weather the colder the water seems to get. One or two well deserve to be named after the saints, although I do not think that any of them has been so named. Until one has drunk from a hill or mountain spring on a warm summer day, one has but a faint notion of what the real taste of water is. Spring water is coldest in summer, while burn water —flowing openly—is coldest in winter.

At the foot of the Green Craigs, just as the Howden Glen is entered, there is a perennial spring. It never failed even during those driest of dry summers, 1911, 1914, and 1918. The mouth is covered with a heavy stone, which visitors should carefully replace after satisfying their thirst. This spring forms part of the inflow to the adjacent collecting cistern, which has the stone over its door with the inscription 'MDCCXC Thoma Elder, Praetor,' and lovers' names in abundance cut in and written on the woodwork of the door. Besides the spring, this cistern is supplied by an intake from the adjacent Howden Burn, and by a pipe from Bonaly Reservoir, nearly a mile away on the other side of the hill to the west. One of the old wooden pipes which brought the first water supply to Edinburgh still lies —or did so a short time ago—on the pipe track between Bonaly Reservoir and the Green Craigs cistern.

On the southern slope of Fala Knowe, just before the ascent of Castlelaw is begun, there is another spring, known as The Colonel's Well. The water is collected into a built tank about two feet square, which has a bottoming of finely broken lava, and an outlet pipe about a foot up from the bottom discharges the water into a stone basin, from which it winds away down the muir to join the Kirk Burn, and so into Glencorse Reservoir to help in supplying the wants of Edinburgh. The water here is of superexcellence—very cool and delicious to the taste. This spring seldom fails, although it did so for a period of many weeks during the dry summer of 1911. In the spring of 1909 it was deeply snowed up from 7th March to 11th April, and even at that late date it was accessible only with difficulty, through a narrow lane some yards long, with snow as high as one's head on either side, like a wall. There is another spring of similar quality, which trickles out of the eastern bank of the Kirk Burn, but it is rather difficult to find.

Good springs are also to be found by the side of the Colinton to Glencorse path, as the descent towards Glencorse is begun ; in the Maiden's Cleuch, Malleny to Glencorse path ; in the Green Cleuch, Balerno to Glencorse path ; and on the Kirk Road from Loganlee to Penicuik ; but the supply to some of these occasionally dries up early in the summer. Another good spring (unfailing, I think) is on the side of the Nine Mile Burn path, where it curves round to the south after leaving the path which descends by Eastside to Silverburn. A very fine spring, well up on the northern slope of Carnethy, to the east of Loganlee Reservoir, rushes out like a little burn from the hillside, and trots down its narrow nick in the hillside to join the stream in the glen.

There is delightful spring water to be drawn from a tap in the embankment near the waterman's cottage at the east end of Harlaw Reservoir. Very cool it is in summer. This water is led from the culvert conveying the Edinburgh water supply from Crosswood, which passes across the embankment at a slightly higher level than this tap. The supply is perennial and abundant. There is also a well in front of the waterman's cottage at the east end of Clubbiedean Reservoir, where a *tinny* is thoughtfully provided for the use of all and sundry.

An excellent supply of good water feeds the trough by the roadside at Bavelaw Castle. For a number of years it was cut off, but it has now been restored. Two other taps, where good drinking water can be had, call for mention ; one at the west end of the steading at Listonshiels, and the other by the side of the path from Currie and Juniper Green, near the shepherd's cottage above Glencorse Reservoir.

While there is no scarcity of water amongst the south-western hills, the great bulk of it appears to be too stagnant to be drinkable. Much of it has a strong vegetable or peaty taste. One must not, however, forget the Rumbling Well, which is situated by the side of the path from West Linton to Dunsyre. This is an excellent drinking water. The rumbling sound is caused by the dropping of the water in the interior of the hill. Lovers of *green meat* will find, in its season, abundance of water-cress growing in the outflow from the well.

On the western shoulder of Caerketton, the hill above Swanston, there is an intermittent spring, which seems to be the 'well water' referred to by

Stevenson in one of his letters from Samoa to his old nurse. 'Some day,' he writes, 'climb as high as Halkerside for me——I am never likely to do it for myself——and sprinkle some of the well water on the turf. I am afraid it is a pagan rite, but quite harmless, and *ye can sain it wi' a bit prayer.*'

There are many other springs about the Pentlands, especially on the slopes that drain into Glencorse and Loganlee reservoirs. Those of us who had to drink the chemically filtered water from Talla on its introduction knew the difference, both in colour and in taste, when Glencorse water was turned on.

Springs and wells of water are favourite meeting and lunching places of hill lovers, and all walkers, after *al fresco* meals, should be particularly careful to remove the evidences of their eating and drinking. To every true walker there is something of worship in his outings. The hills to him are holy temples, and there is nothing more offensive than, on arriving at one of these springs——shrines, might one say ?—— to find the outflow choked with paper or cardboard boxes, and the ground littered with orange and banana skins, broken bottles, and such like. It is so easy, too, to dispose of these things. They can be covered with stones, pushed into holes, or mole hillocks, or hidden under a heather bush. Will all readers who are walkers please note ? They should also remember that broken glass is very dangerous to both sheep and dogs.

The only natural loch within the area of the Pentlands is the little Crane Loch, which lies almost at the south-western extremity of the hills, and near to the Twin Laws, one of which is so slight an eminence that its green top may be ascended from the surrounding muirland in about twenty steps. Viewed from this slight eminence, the Crane Loch looks like a veritable eye of the wilderness. Closer acquaintanceship, however, dispels any such romantic imaginings. To approach its irregular-shaped edge seems the easiest thing in the world, but, except in very dry weather, it is the reverse of easy. The loch, it is evident, had at one time a considerably larger area than it has at present. The flat approaches to it are water-logged, and, for almost the whole year, cannot be traversed with dry feet. It is treacherous ground too, dotted with seemingly hard grassy tufts, from one to another of which an active man can leap, to find comparatively dry footing. But every tuft is not hard and grassy. Many of them turn out to be of sphagnum moss, into which the foot sinks, while the moss closes over the top of the boot, in a way quite beautiful to look at, and the water is squeezed as if from a sponge, and percolates insidiously to the soles of the feet. The loch is irregular in shape; and perhaps one could walk round it in from one to two hundred paces. Even this small area is being encroached on. The western end is silting up, and it is easily seen that the loch is undergoing the process which all such lochs undergo, that of being absorbed by the land.

The name Crane Loch would most likely be given to it from cranes, or perhaps herons, having at one time frequented it. Instead of cranes or herons, there is now, in the spring time, a colony of black-headed gulls nesting amongst the ooze and aquatic plants and grasses. Their nests, on the occasion of one of my visits, were very numerous—some in course of construction, and others each with one greenish-gray egg in it. The ground round the edge of the water is exceedingly dirty, and the loch conveys the best impression when viewed from a little distance.

One always has an interest, somewhat boyish it may be, but none the less enjoyable on that account, in following up boundaries between countries or counties; in noting what form the dividing lines, and how they converge or separate. The boundaries of the counties of Midlothian, Lanark, and Peebles

Boundaries and Habitation.
meet in the very heart of the hills, in the Medwin valley, between the peaks know as The Pike, White Craig, and Millstone Rig. The walker may stand with one foot in Midlothian, the other in Peebles, and place his stick in Lanark—that is, provided he has been endowed by nature with sufficient length of leg to stride across the little stream, which comes hurrying down the Raven's Cleuch from Craigengar, and joins the Medwin water just where the county boundaries meet. The boundary lines follow the courses of these two little streams.

One hardly fancies taking up his abode permanently on any of the wide tracts of rather wet inhospitable muirland which are here and there to be found amongst the Pentlands, as amongst most hills; and yet there is evidence in at least one place-name that the Pentlands, in the far distant past it is true, have not been without permanent habitations. The tract of muirland stretching from the Hare Hill and the West Kip to the bases of the East Cairn Hill and Wether Law is known as the Kitchen Moss, presumably from the primitive remains called Kitchen Middens which have been found in it. These doubtless indicate the presence, at one time, of a comparatively extensive population on this high bare muir. Dr Milne, in his book *Place Names of Midlothian*, says that the name is derived from the Gaelic, and signifies 'moss of the little fold.' There are, however, indications of human habitation which cannot be gainsaid—the foundations of old houses. In the howe at Loganlee some grass-grown old walls are traceable, while on the bank of the burn, beyond the waterfall, the remains of Hare Hill House can still be plainly seen—the garden ground extending down the bank to the burn side. During recent excavations pieces of coarse pottery or stoneware were found in what had doubtless been the house midden.

The little burn which takes its rise in the Kitchen Moss, and has cut its narrow bed through the peat and the boulder clay to tumble so picturesquely through the gorge and over the rocks at Loganlee, boasted at one time three names in its short course, before it emptied its waters into the North Esk river. It started as the Kitchen Burn; when it emerged from Loganlee Reservoir it was the Logan Burn; and finally, in its course between Glencorse Reservoir and the North Esk, it was the Glencorse Burn. It still retains the last two names.

In hilly and mountainous districts an interesting feature is always to be found in the waterfalls and cascades on the little burns as they hurry down

from the hills to the glens and cleuchs. The
waterfalls of the Pentlands are not grand. They
Waterfalls
and
Gorges. are moderate in volume and fall, but some
of them are exceedingly pretty. Most
Edinburgh people are familiar with them.
The one best known is situated about half a mile
up the glen from Loganlee Reservoir, at the spot
still known to many people—although wrongly it
would appear—as Habbie's Howe. Another is on
the little burn between Torduff and Clubbiedean
reservoirs, beyond Colinton, on the north side of the
hills. A third is on the south side of the hills
at Patie's Mill, Carlops, in the neighbourhood of
the now accepted Habbie's Howe.

These are pretty waterfalls, as has been said.
There is another, however, which might without
any exaggeration be called grand. It is in the glen
immediately to the east of Glencorse Reservoir, and
is formed by the overflow from it. It is therefore
intermittent, and really only exists when the reservoir is full and overflowing. At such a time the
white foam can be descried through the bare trees
from far up the slope of Turnhouse Hill. To my
mind this is quite as fine a waterfall as some of
those which have acquired national celebrity—the
Grey Mare's Tail and the Falls of Foyers, for instance.
In similar circumstances the overflow from Harlaw
Reservoir is almost equally fine, though not so
natural. There is first a rapid rush of water over
a steep slope—a water-slide which even the redoubt-
able John Ridd would have found difficult to climb,
then a sudden leap of ten or twelve feet, a miniature
Niagara, succeeded by five other lesser falls, over

which the water dashes with much noise and spray.

The foregoing remarks apply to the waterfalls when in their normal condition. The one at Loganlee is, perhaps, a foot or two in breadth, and has cut its narrow channel through the rocks. But I have seen it after a spring thaw, on a wet foggy day, when the peaty-coloured water, churned into foam, extended from side to side of the rocky chasm, and, viewed through the mist, appeared to be issuing from the clouds.

There are several pretty little falls of perhaps from six to twelve feet in height; one on a tributary of the Logan Burn, a little way beyond the waterfall before mentioned; and two or three on the burns amongst the south-western hills—tiny thread-like trickles for the most part, but making a rare music to the ear of him who will be at the trouble to go and seek them out.

The short gorge immediately to the east of Glencorse Reservoir is a place of singular beauty, both in its configuration and in the seasonal adornments which Nature bestows upon it. The banks, thickly covered with trees and studded with rocky knobs, slope steeply down into a narrow bottom, scarcely more than sufficient for the little stream to glide in. A shelter from the storm, there is warmth there even on the wildest winter day; a shadow from the heat, there is coolness in the fiercest of the dogdays, and a subdued, softened, hazy atmosphere, reminding one of the dim religious light of vast cathedral aisles. Spring brings star-like primroses to adorn the banks; summer the foxglove spires of purple; autumn the glowing gold to the maples, and the ruddy brown to the beeches; while winter brings a drapery of snow to the Scots firs and the spruces, and icicles, reflecting rainbow colours, to the waterfall.

Right in the heart of the hills, on the border between Midlothian and Peebles, is a curious flow moss, which looks for all the world like a green glacier. It was known more than two hundred years ago as the Deer Slunk, and appears to have altered but little since that time. More than likely the motion is in the water only, but the green moss *appears* also to be moving. During wet weather, or after the melting of a heavy snowfall, the Deer Slunk is one of the most difficult parts of the Pentlands to negotiate.

Carlops Dean and the Windy Gowl together form a very remarkable feature. They are 'a trough nearly straight, and about two miles long,' the bottom, of the Dean at least, 'everywhere a marsh or wet meadow.' This trough runs from north-east to south-west, and the Dean, which is at the north-east end, is considerably the wider and deeper part of the trough bottom, being perhaps one hundred and fifty yards in width, and of considerable depth. In the centre of the Dean is a broken ridge known as Dun Kaim, while to the north of this ridge is an isolated, conical, grass-covered mound, similar to the moats at Hawick and Carnwath, but without the trees as at Carnwath. More to the south-west rises another isolated cone, rocky in this instance, known as the Peaked Craig. Adjoining the Peaked Craig, at the foot of Mount Maw, is what is popularly spoken of

Caves and Rocks.

as a cave, an excavation out of the solid rock of the hill mass. It is known alternatively as Jenny Barry's Cove and Hell's Hole. Certainly, on a dull day, the entrance is black enough to fit all the traditions which cluster around the latter name. It is between four and five feet high, and on the occasion of the writer's first visit to it, a bleak day in November, there was a considerable amount of water covering the rocky floor, making the exploration of the cave somewhat difficult. Rough *coggly* stepping-stones about four or five yards inwards enabled a survey to be made for that distance, and by tossing in stones an estimate could be formed that the cave extended at least as far again. A big stone, dropped into an apparent hole immediately beyond our standpoint, indicated by its splash a considerable depth of water. A little to the south-west of the cave the Dean ends, narrowing into the Windy Gowl, which looks, as Mr Reith very aptly remarks in *The Breezy Pentlands*, 'like a long straight sword cut in the hills.' The name gowl without doubt signifies gully.

To the north-east of the Peaked Craig are traces of an old curling-pond, with several broken curling-stones lying amongst the rushes and aquatic grasses that now flourish on the side of the pond. The Linn Burn, coming down from Carlops Hill, forms a series of picturesque little cascades as it tumbles between the rocks in its haste to join the Carlops Burn.

Chambers, in his *History of Peeblesshire*, mentions Jenny Barry's Cove and Hell's Hole as two separate places of interest in the Dean—the Cove on the north-east side, and Hell's Hole on the south-east side.

We—there were four in the party—saw but the one cave, a most likely place certainly to be called Hell's Hole, while in the village we heard the name of Jenny Barry's Cove applied to the same place. Since this first visit I have explored the Dean and the Windy Gowl thoroughly several times, and I am perfectly satisfied that there is only one cave in it. It is generally believed that the excavation had been made in the course of mining operations for lead and silver. It is perhaps possible that a slight depression on the south-east side of the Windy Gowl may be the Hell's Hole referred to by Chambers; but if so, the name seems strangely inappropriate.

Windy Gowl and Carlops Dean, with their earth and rock mounds and kaims, have probably been formed by the action of the glacier ice, which ploughed out the trough-like valley, and left the harder rocky mound standing up so boldly from the bottom of the Dean. The kaim has been formed, more than likely, by the deposit, by the glacier, of rocks and other material which it had forced with it in its passage through the Windy Gowl. Dun Kaim would indicate the occupation, during early historic times, of the ridgy, broken mound as a fort. Charles Maclaren, in his book on the geology of the Pentlands, concludes that these changes were brought about by water sweeping away the sandstone strata and leaving the harder rocky mounds upstanding in the Dean.

The Bore Stane is a somewhat striking and curious-looking outcrop of rock on the summit of the path which connects Balerno and Midcalder, on the north side of the hills, with Carlops on the south side. The rocks are situated a little to the west of the path and indicate the most northerly point of a tongue, or wedge, which the county of Peebles thrusts into Midlothian. There is nothing about this Bore Stane which might lead one to infer that it had been used for a purpose similar to the other two Bore Stanes in Scotland, the one in Morningside Road, Edinburgh, with its memories of Flodden, and the other

The Bore Stane.

at Bannockburn; nor does there seem to be any record of a muster of troops at this out-of-the-way spot. It has occurred to me that the name may have arisen through this point having been used as a station from which to take sights during some early survey of the district. The expression to bore is still used in this sense by building tradesman in various districts of Scotland. The position of these rocks, too, it seems to me, gives support to such a theory. Situated on the watershed of the district, at the apex, so to speak, of the county of Peebles, and affording extensive views to both north and south, it is a perfect spot from which long sights can be taken, and the relative positions of various natural features determined.

Most of the hills are, of course, pastoral, and

afford but poor pasturage during a good part of the
year.   Portions of them have, however, been brought
Pastures under cultivation, and are either cropped,
Green.   or in grass, at heights ranging from 750
to 1000 feet above sea-level.   In some of the glens
there are little patches in the vicinity of shepherds'
houses, where potatoes, cabbages, and other garden
produce have been grown up to about that height.
These patches are mostly unfenced, and at a little
distance are undistinguishable from the surrounding
muirland.   There are evidences of an old cultivation
at various places amongst the hills ; for example,
near Bavelaw, and on the muir on the north side of
West Kip.   At the latter place an area of ground
is still partially enclosed by old *flae* (turf) dykes,
which are known locally as Gordon's Dykes.   The
rigs are very narrow, much rounded in the centre,
and the furrows are correspondingly deep.   This
arrangement was made for drainage purposes, and
improved the ground very much when it was in
crop, although it is said that when the land was in
grass the furrow was a dangerous place for a sheep
to get 'awalt' in, that is, on its back.   There is, I
understand, no difficulty in this high-rounded rig
and deep-furrow formation being obtained by plough-
ing, although some authorities contend that in most
cases the spade has been the implement used.

It is mainly the hardy, black-faced, horned sheep
that are adaptable to these hills.   Occasionally a few
cattle during summer, when grass is plentiful, obtain
fair pasturage about the muirs and the slopes of
the glens ; while immediately before harvest some
farmers, when there is nothing for horses to do,

turn them out for a few weeks to roam over the hill portions of their farms.

The curious sight of a sheep eating out of one's hand I have more than once seen, at different parts of the hills. At one time there were at least three ewes which were thus sociable. Their lambs did not, however, develop the same friendly habits. These three sheep were 'Hail, fellow! well met' with anyone who liked to treat them. They did not stand on ceremony, but in the most insistent manner poked their noses into one's rucksack, or into the paper bag out of which one was eating. Nothing there came amiss to them, from bread-and-butter to apples or mutton sandwiches, so that even such a mild-mannered creature as a sheep has, like man, the seeds of cannibalism in its nature. One of them was a regular highwayman, adopting a policy of stand and deliver towards every tramper lunching near its feeding-ground.

The Pentlands are not a happy hunting-ground for the archæologist. Ruins and other objects of antiquarian interest are few. Possibly the oldest remains are those of the church of St

Antiquities. Catherine of the Hopes, which, with its churchyard, is submerged by the waters of Glencorse Reservoir. These remains have been laid bare several times, much oftener than most people are aware of, by the shrinkage of the waters in the summer and autumn months. The ruins show the church to have been forty feet long by twenty feet wide, and the walls are said to be about eighteen inches high, with a hewn corner at the south-west angle. It is also recorded (see Cochrane's *Pentland Walks*) that 'there is a tombstone at the south-east corner six feet long by three feet four inches wide, with a plain shield in the middle, below that a date of 1623, and part of an inscription at the bottom of the lettering, which evidently reads, "Blessed are the dead who die in the Lord."' It is further stated that, 'In a letter in the *Scotsman* in 1898, another tombstone is referred to as a boulder-protected tombstone erected to the memory of James Glendinning, bearing the date 1666,' the year of the battle of Rullion Green. The church, it is said, had not been used for two hundred years prior to 1842.

In 1915, when the present writer last saw this ruin, the walls were only 'a rickle o' stanes,' and certainly not eighteen inches high. There were traces of good hard lime-mortar here and there, but no sign of a hewn corner at the south-west angle. The boulder-protected tombstone was there, the boulder protection being modern work, but the inscription was illegible. This tombstone was lying flat at the south-east angle of the ruin, and was the only tombstone visible. Traces of what might have been the graveyard wall were also discernible to the south of the ruins of the church.

Logan Tower.

In all probability, now that a branch from the Talla Water supply has been led into Glencorse, the ruins of this old church may never again be seen.

Logan Tower, a little farther up the glen, between

Glencorse and Loganlee reservoirs, and almost hidden amongst the trees by which it is surrounded, is evidently a sixteenth-century erection—an example of a small square peel tower. The date 1230, said to have been cut at one time on a lintel, is an altogether preposterous one.

The old ruin standing so picturesquely on the rocky knoll, overlooking the little burn, which comes brattling down from near the top of the Big Black Hill and enters Loganlee Reservoir about midway from each end, is popularly known as Hoolet's Hoose. The suggestion that this ruin may be the remains of the house of the priest connected with St Catherine's Chapel is plausible, although I am disposed to think that it is the remains of an old baronial building somewhat after the style of Logan Tower. Evidently it is of considerable age, and the ground floor has been vaulted over. Part of the vaulting still remains. Mr Cochrane states that the vaulting was entire in 1877. 'It is to be hoped,' he adds, 'that the remains will be preserved.' At the time of writing, nothing has been done, nor seems likely to be done, towards their preservation. In 'Gellatly's New Map of the country twelve miles round Edinburgh, drawn by William Johnston, Land Surveyor,' published in 1834, this ruin is noted as an 'old chapel.' The building has probably been occupied within comparatively recent times—as long as walls and roof could be got to hold together—by a shepherd, or other farm or estate worker. Then, when the roof began to leak, and the walls to bulge, it has been vacated and left to fall into decay. This has been the common fate of many of these old

baronial buildings. There are traces of the foundations of an outhouse, and also of walls which had
enclosed a small garden, on the westward side of the
old ruin.

The stone lying on the summit of Monk's Rig,
close to the Monk's Road, and marked on the map as
Font Stone, is not, nor has it ever been, a font. The
first sight of it determines that. The stone is a
basaltic boulder; whether native or erratic I cannot
say, but I incline to think it is an erratic. Its area
is roughly three feet by two and a half feet, with
a thickness of from twelve to fifteen inches. In the
top of the stone there is a deepish wedge-shaped
sinking, which may, quite easily, have been the
socket for the shaft of a cross; and at one of the
longer sides of the top there are two slight depressions, which may also have been meant for, or
have been hollowed by, the knees of the traveller
worshippers—but if so, then the shaft of the cross
must have been clasped by the worshipper. Perhaps
this formed part of the act of worship.

In all probability the stone is lying at, or near, its
original position. It weighs some ten or twelve

Font Stone (so called),
Monk's Road.

hundredweights, so that the
shifting of it would not be a
job to be lightly undertaken.
In mediæval times, crosses
were erected on the main roads
leading to monasteries and
abbeys, just where the first
view of the sacred building

was obtained. Presuming that there was a monastery
at Newhall, as tradition asserts there was, this stone

lies exactly where the first view of the monastery would be obtained by anyone travelling to it over the Monk's Road from, say, Queensferry or any of the adjacent Forth ports; so that possibly this stone has been the base of a cross, instead of a font stone.

Brown, in his *Notes on Pennicuik*, states that 'the ornamental top of the cross is still lying at the foot of the rig.' I presume this means that the cross was of stone. I find it somewhat hard to believe that a stone cross could be shaped and fitted into the socket so as to be secure. It would certainly be very poor construction. I am inclined to think that the cross must have been made of wood, which could be shaped and jammed, or wedged, into the socket in a way that stone could not be. A cross of wood could also be shored or strutted, and it would require some support of this description in such a bare exposed situation. But, after all is said, the stone may be only a drinking-trough! The present owner of Newhall is of opinion that there has not been a monastery there.

The old church at Glencorse, with its memories of Stevenson, is not really amongst the Pentlands; neither is the church at Currie; and these are, therefore, only referred to here. Nor is more than mention necessary of the Lennox Tower in the valley of the Water of Leith, Craiglockhart Tower, and Colinton Castle.

Most people find it hard to believe that Bavelaw Castle is an ancient house; it is in such excellent preservation. In the usual acceptation of the name castle, as implying a building for offence or defence, Bavelaw can hardly lay claim to the title. It was

originally more in the nature of a hunting lodge.
The date of its erection is not known, but from its
architectural features, competent authorities have been led to place it some time
during the sixteenth century. Evidently the original
entrance roadway was from the east. There are two
gate pillars on that
side of the grounds,
and an old road
from Edinburgh
can be plainly
traced across the
muir towards this
entrance. Altera-
tions and additions
were made to the old house in 1912, without
detracting from its characteristically Scottish appearance, but most people would, no doubt, have been
better pleased had it been left in its original condition. In Gellatly's 1834 map the name is spelled
Bevelaw, meaning perhaps Cattle
Law.

Bavelaw Castle.

The only other ruin to which
reference requires to be made is
that of East Cairns Castle,
which is situated at the south-
west end of Harper Rig Reservoir.
It is also believed to be a sixteenth
century erection, but practically
nothing is known of its history.
It is in a very dilapidated condition, and, if left
alone, will in a few years be little more than a heap
of stones. It may probably, as is alleged, have

Cairns Castle.

been erected as a menace to the Border thieves—
Scotts and Douglases, Elliots, Armstrongs, and
Rutherfords (from the last mentioned of whom I
am myself descended)—who were in the habit of
coming through the Cauld Stane Slap to harry the
rich Lothian lands and lift cattle.

Fairly extensive quarrying operations have been
carried on at various parts of the hills in past days,
most likely for material with which to build the
drystone dykes forming the fences between different
properties. A few quarries are still worked, but
only for road metal. At Ravelrig, which is on the
outskirts of the hills, the well-known Ravelrig
paving setts are quarried. Walkers on the outlook
for antiquities need not go to the top of Hare Hill
in quest of such. The mounds there, which look
so like old forts or tumuli, are in reality the rubbish
heaps from a disused quarry on the top of the hill.

It is said that a certain Michael Lining, an
Edinburgh lawyer, who owned portions of the hills
during the latter part of the eighteenth century,
offered to supply, free of cost, a sufficiency of stone
from the Cairn Hills wherewith to complete the
so-called National Monument on the Calton Hill
at Edinburgh. Michael Lining was secretary of
the committee entrusted with the erection of the
monument. It is a moot point, however, whether
any stone suitable for such a purpose could have
been got out of the Cairn Hills, although there are
several *faces* where good stone, to all appearance,
could be quarried. This Michael Lining seems to
have been a man somewhat in advance of the age
in which he lived, as it is also recorded of him that

he had a project for manufacturing fuel out of peat, and had erected some buildings for that purpose on the moss near Colzium. It is stated by John Geddie, in his *Water of Leith*, that a stone chimney-stalk forming part of this manufactory was shattered by a storm so lately as 1884, and that a portion of it was still standing quite recently. I have not been able to locate the position of these buildings.

A little to the south of West Bavelaw there is an old building, which has evidently been used as a lime-kiln. It is mounded up on its east side so that stone and fuel could be tipped in there, and in the opposite wall there is the usual arched opening where the lime and ashes could be drawn out. In the immediate neighbourhood there are evidences of workings from which material of some sort has been removed. It looks as if lime had been burned there in the past. Dr Peach, of the Geological Survey, says that 'a band of cornstone lying near the base of the sandstones was formerly worked for lime' at this place, and also in the Ravendean and the Baddingsgill burns.

Most of the paths, or rights of way, across the hills are now merely foot-tracks, more or less clearly defined, but, without question, they were originally well-used roads. In the main they are natural pathways from one side of the hills to the other, and, what every good road should do, they follow the line of least resistance. Several of the paths, as they approach the main roads, are distinctly *made*; but even in the very heart of the hills there are, here and there, notably where the path from Balerno to Carlops

Paths and Rights of Way.

crosses the Kitchen Moss, distinct evidences of *making*, the material used being rounded water-worn pebbles, taken from the adjoining burn no doubt. In various places the paths have been nicked out of the hillsides, and a certain amount of *making* has consequently been bestowed on them at these places also.

The path from Balerno to Carlops is carried across the Logan or Kitchen Burn by a bridge, which, while there is nothing about it to fix its age definitely, has evidently conveyed many generations across the little stream, and seen much water run underneath its arch. This bridge is remarkably like those said to have been erected by General Wade, spanning the streams on the Corriyarrick Pass.

The recognised paths across the hills are so carefully described in the various guide-books dealing with the Pentlands, and so accurately delineated on the maps (referred to later), that it is unnecessary to do more than merely mention them here.

Every true lover of the hills blesses, in his heart if not by audible speech, the men and women of old time who established and maintained these rights of way. But for them we should now, undoubtedly, be absolutely shut out from the hills. They deserve, more than many, that some lasting memorial should be raised to their memory; but failing this, every tramper who follows in their footsteps can raise a memorial of gratitude to them in his own heart, and see to it that the old ways are kept open, and that none of the adjuncts are filched from us, nor the amenity of the paths inter-

fered with in any way. In this connection I cannot
help saying that the action of the Edinburgh
Merchant Company in enclosing the Colinton path
with ugly wire fences, and thus compelling walkers,
during wet weather, to slide or skate down the
path as best they may, is not likely to inspire
grateful memories in the heart of any hill lover.

In the opinion of the writer, the Pentlands are
the finest range for hill-walking in the neighbourhood of Edinburgh. The Lammermuirs he would
place as a good second, and the Moorfoots as a
somewhat indifferent third. The Moorfoot range includes at least two peaks which are higher than
any in the Pentlands, but, with some few exceptions,
all the hills of the Moorfoot range are so softly
rounded that their appearance is homely in the
extreme, and, speaking generally, they are not nearly
so dry as the Pentlands or the Lammermuirs, while
the Lammermuirs are neither so high nor so steep
as the Pentlands. In one respect the Lammermuirs
do excel, and that is in the abundance of heather
with which they are covered ; indeed, they are
perhaps the most heathery hills in Scotland.

As was stated in the Preface, this is not intended
to be a guide-book. There seems to be a sufficiency
of these already. The writer would advise the
prospective hill-walker to provide himself with a
Bartholomew's or a Johnston's map. These maps are
excellent in every respect. Get one mounted on cloth,
for, as some writer has said, 'Fooling about with
a paper map in a high wind is a sure way of learn-
ing profanity !' And that is a practice which should
not be indulged in amongst the holy places of the

hills. The larger scale map (inch-and-a-half to the mile) of the Pentland area is, perhaps, the best for walking purposes; the smaller scale ones (half-inch to the mile) may be referred to for verifying the outlook from the hills.

LEGEND AND HISTORY.

VARIOUS attempts have been made to define the origin and meaning of the name Pentland. Most writers, following Skene, have accepted *Pehtland,* meaning 'the land of the Picts,' as the original name; but more recent historical writers seem to be of opinion that the Picts did not obtain a footing in the neighbourhood of the Pentlands until a comparatively late date—viz., after the departure of the Romans; and even then their occupation appears to have been but partial, and for a short time. It seems unlikely, in such circumstances, that these hills should have been specially named Pictlands, when the lands occupied by the Picts for so many centuries were to the north of the Forth. Later writers on place-names have, therefore, been induced to seek for a different derivation of the name.

Origin of the Name.

In *Place Names of Scotland* (1903), the Rev. J. B. Johnston hazards the guess that a probable reference is to the hills penning in the Penicuik valley. *Pin* and *pen,* he says, are from the same root; and he refers his readers to the Scottish word *pend,* as in a *pend* close—but one fails to see the connection, a pend close being a covered close.

Another writer derives the name from two Cymric words, *penn laun,* signifying 'height over the enclosed land.' *Laun,* he says, is 'cognate with land, and is so spelt in Icelandic, Danish, and Old Gaelic.'

Dr Milne, in his effort to derive all Midlothian place-names from the Gaelic, hazards *beinn* (pronounced ben), 'hill,' and *lamham* (pronounced lan), also 'hill'; and adds that a euphonic (*t*) had been added to *beinn* and a euphonic (*d*) to *lamham*. That is to say that Pentland is simply 'hill, hill.' Had the separate words composing the name been derived from different languages, one could have understood; but that two different words, each signifying the same thing and derived from the same language, should have been joined to name a range of hills is surely most unlikely.

Mr Edmund McClure, M.A., in his *British Place Names in their Historical Setting* (1910), says: '*Pen* is a distinctly British word, corresponding to the Gaelic *ceann*, or *ken*—anciently *cend*—and signifying a head.' The prefix *pen* occurs in various hill names, particularly in southern Scotland, as for instance in the Southern Uplands, Ettrick Pen, Skelfhill Pen, Penchrise Pen, and others. Isaac Taylor, in his well-known *Words and Places*, singles out the Pentland Hills as an example in *pen* of the Cymric form of the word.

It is never quite safe to dogmatise on such a matter as a place-name, because, frequently, names have become so corrupted during the course of centuries as to have lost not only their original meanings but also their original sounds. 'Headlands,' however, seems to be an altogether appropriate name for a range of hills, and there is a strong presumption that this interpretation is correct. There is an evident close connection between the words *pen* and *ben*, and the likelihood is that

they are respectively the Cymric (or British) and
the Gaelic names for a hill or mountain, and that the
addition, perhaps at a later date, of the word *land*
to the earlier word *pen* explains the origin of the
name Pentland, the *t* being inserted (perhaps at a
still later date) for the sake of euphony, or 'added
by ignorance,' as Chalmers sarcastically says in his
Caledonia about the *d* in Cramond, the Caer Amon
of the Romans.   The word *land* seems to have been
used in its modern acceptation by all the primitive
peoples who inhabited Europe.

Skene—very arbitrarily, it seems to me—in his
contention that the name is corrupted from *Pehtland*
says that it was applied to the hills by the Angles,
who held the adjacent country to the south-east.
The Pentland Hills, he admits, formed the *boundary*
of the territory occupied by the Picts—occupied,
as we have seen, at a late date, partially and tem-
porarily.   It would, I think, be more likely that the
name was given by the Brythonic Celts, who lived
in the district centuries before the Picts set foot in
it.   It must also be borne in mind that the name
Pict, or Picti, meaning tatooed or painted men, was
very widely applied by the Romans, who Latinised
it from the Celtic *Pehta*, or *Peicta*, the fighters.

Altogether, it appears to me that McClure's derivation of the name is the most reasonable of any put
forward.

Whether the Romans ever occupied the Pentland
Hills may be disputed, but there can hardly be a
doubt that the tramp of the legions must often have
been heard past their north-eastern end.   The Roman
Watling Street, their great main north road from

London, went that way to Cramond. Passing through
the Cheviot Hills at Chew Green, where there is a
Roman very fine example of a Roman station,
Roads and now known by the misleading modern
Camps. name of Ad Fines, the great road crossed
Kale Water at Towford; Oxnam Water near
Cappuck; and the river Teviot at Jedfoot, where,
for a distance of six or seven miles either way, it
still runs, as a modern highway, in an almost straight
line, direct to the great camp at Newstead. Crossing
the Tweed there, it inclined to the west, and, in all
probability, passed along the high ground between
the Gala and Allan Waters to Soutra. Thereafter it
seems to have crossed the Gore Water at Borthwick
Castle; the South Esk at Dalhousie; the North Esk
at Mavisbank; and then proceeded by Loanhead past
the end of the Pentlands to Cramond, where there
was a Roman port. From Cramond the road went
by Queensferry and Abercorn to Carriden at the
eastern end of the great wall of Antoninus. It
seems to have been subsequently extended to Perth.

It is said by Codrington (in *Roman Roads in
Britain*) that at the end of the eighteenth century
the road was plainly visible for more than a mile
north from Lothianburn. Possibly the humble little
bridge which spans the burn at Bowbridge, about
fifteen or sixteen feet below the level of the present
roadway, carried the famous street across the Lothian
Burn. The course of the street northwards would
most probably be by the square-shaped strip of wood
adjacent to the standing-stone by the side of the
road leading from Fairmilehead to Hunter's Tryst.
There are two old maps in the Royal Scottish

Museum, both of which indicate a Roman camp near the site mentioned. The first is entitled 'A Plan of Edinburgh from an actual survey delineated by John Lawrie, Geographer. Published according to Act of Parliament by William Creech, Edinburgh 1811.' This 'plan' shows the road passing through a camp a little to the north of Fairmilehead. The other map or plan is a much better example of the map-maker's art, and was 'Published by John Thomson and Co. 1822.' On it the camp is shown at the trees previously mentioned. Personally, I should say there are indications of a camp having been there.

Perhaps it is also worth noting that one of the names of the standing-stone is the Caie Stone, and that Caiaphas and Caius were Roman names. There may be some connection between these names and the name of the stone.

Causewayend, near Harper Rig Reservoir, marks, in all probability, the termination of another Roman road. Names in which the word causeway occurs are now generally accepted by archæologists as indicating the presence (at or near them) of a Roman highway. The existence of a camp on Camilty Hill, about two miles south-west of Causewayend, the fragments of Roman pottery, and the coins of Vespasian, Hadrian, and Marcus Aurelius, which have been dug up at this place, are undeniable evidence of the presence of the Romans, and, at the same time, circumstantial evidence of the existence of a roadway, either round the northern skirts of the Pentlands or across country from the Firth of Forth.

The path across the Pentlands from Currie (which is identified by some writers as a Roman station)

passes down the Maiden Cleuch to Glencorse.
Codrington in his book, previously quoted, says that
the name Maiden Way is distinctly a Roman name.
It is, therefore, quite probable that the word maiden
in Maiden Cleuch is a survival from Roman times.

East Cairn Hill from Maiden Cleuch Path.

The name Maiden Well-brow, on the Lang Whang,
near Tarbrax, may also indicate the presence there
of the old world conquerors.

The name Black Birns, as applied to a hill a little
south of Tarbrax, may also indicate the presence of
a Roman camp, although it has to be noted that the
word *birns* is, in Lowland Scotland, applied to the
dried, withered stems of dead or burned heather.   It
may also be noted, however, that inscribed stones,
proving a Roman occupation, have been found at
Birrens in Dumfriesshire, and it has been said that
the name indicates the existence of such stones.

Undoubtedly the Britons have left traces of their

occupation of the Pentlands in at least three camps
or forts : one on the east side of Castlelaw ; another
British   fully a mile to the south-west, on the
Forts.   southern slope of Turnhouse Hill ; and a
third on Camp Hill, near the southern termination of
the Kirk Road at Silverburn.   These are referred
to in the description of the hills where they are
situated.   It seems to me that we have also traces
of the Britons in the immense piles of stones on the
summits of some of the peaks, and in the names of
these peaks.   The Craigs and Cairns speak of the
occupancy by a Celtic people, either British or Gaelic,
just as the various Laws and Hills testify to the
presence of the Anglo-Saxons.   Composite names,
such as Scald Law, for instance, seem to point to a
successive early occupancy by two different peoples.

The prefix *Cat* in Catstone Hill undoubtedly
indicates the site of some prehistoric battle, Catstone
signifying battle rock.   Deerhope Rig as surely
refers to the former presence of the wild animal
named amongst the adjacent hills and hopes ; just as
the bones of the reindeer found in the rock fissures
at the Green Craigs near Dreghorn imply the former
existence of Arctic conditions, so amply confirmed by
the contours of most of the hills.

The presence of the base of a cross, already
referred to, on the summit of Monk's Rig, between
Braid Law and Spital Hill, and the occurrence of
Monks   such names as Spital Hill, Monk's Burn,
and   Monk's Rig, Monk's Haugh, and Friarton,
Templars. undoubtedly indicate the existence, in
mediæval times, of monastic buildings in the neighbourhood.   Tradition has located these at Newhall,

which is a little distance to the south of the places named. If, as the present proprietor asserts, there has not been a monastery at Newhall, there must have been such an institution at no great distance from it.

The great semi-military religious order of the Templars possessed considerable tracts of land on, and in the neighbourhood of, the Pentland Hills between the twelfth and sixteenth centuries. Traces of their occupancy are to be found in various place-names of which the word Temple forms a part, and in the gravestone with the long straight sword, the emblem of the Templars, cut on it, in Currie churchyard.

Marchbanks, between Balerno and Bavelaw, is said to have been the patrimony of Marjorie, the daughter of Robert the Bruce—hence the name Marjoribanks, pronounced Marchbanks. Listonshiels, up to the time of the Reformation, when it was grabbed by one or other of our greedy Scottish noblemen, was owned by the church of Kirkliston, an old name of which was Templeliston, another indication of the presence of the Templars.

Without doubt such paths as those by the Cauld Stane Slap, the Bore Stane, and the Nine Mile Burn were originally main roads. There is distinct evidence in places that they have been both *made* and kept. The Cauld Stane Slap path, in particular, is a natural highway between Lothian and Tweed-dale and on to the Border Marches. John Geddie, in his *Water of Leith*, quotes from old papers to show that, during the lawless times of the sixteenth century, the path through 'the Slap' was the route by which the 'broken men' of the Borders, who had 'schakin of all fear of God, reverence of the law, and regaird of honestie,' made their raids, even from far-off Eskdale and Liddesdale, into the fertile Lothians.

In his contest with the Scottish Parliament, Cromwell and his troops had a camp 'on Pentland Hills'—'towards Colington'—both in 1650 and in 1651, on which latter occasion one of his officers informed him that the soldiers 'eate bisketts and cheese on Pentland Hills.' In 1650 he had also a camp at Galachlaw, from which place he wrote a letter to Leslie on 14th August. Galachlaw is a slight eminence a little to the east of Fairmilehead, and just outside the Pentland area. It is on the estate of Mortonhall, on the north side of the road leading from Fairmilehead to Liberton by way of Kaims, and almost opposite to the steading of Morton Mains. I fancy that some lines of an encampment are still traceable, between Caerketton and Allermuir Hill, and also a little farther west, which may indicate the site of Cromwell's camps 'on Pentland Hills' 'towards Colington.'

Rullion Green, on the eastern side of Turnhouse Hill, recalls unhappy memories. The battle fought there on 28th November 1666 is, perhaps, the best authenticated and most important historical The Covenanters. event which has occurred within the Pentland area. The site of the battle is immediately adjacent to the Biggar Road, and the memorial stone, referred to elsewhere, will be found at the edge of a wood, a field's breadth from the road, near the summit of the long steep slope from Flotterstone Bridge.

The Covenanting army, more a rabble than an army—certainly not an army in the sense in which we now use the word—was composed largely of West Country Whigs. They were marching from Bathgate to Edinburgh, and had reached Colinton on the evening of that surly, sleety 27th of November, when word was brought to their leader, bearing the great name of Wallace, that the Cowgate port in Edinburgh was secured against them, and that they could not be admitted to the city. An attack seems to have been made upon them during the night, with what result is not very clear.

In the early morning the order to march was given, and finding their way to Edinburgh barred they commenced their retreat to the west country, a bedraggled and somewhat undisciplined crowd, variously estimated at from 900 to 3000 strong, by way of the north-eastern end of the Pentlands. With Dalyell and his troopers in pursuit, and the country people mostly hostile, there was no other course open to them. The fates, however, were not propitious. Dalyell, taking the path across the Pentlands from Currie, and, evidently from the accounts, keeping well up on the shoulder of Turnhouse Hill, where the course of the old road seems to have been, was just in time to intercept them as they halted at Gallowlaw to allow their stragglers to come up. Notwithstanding an initial advantage to the Covenanters, there could only be one result to such an unequal conflict. They appear to have been led with both skill and courage, and to have shown much better fighting qualities than might have been expected of them, but in the end they were routed utterly; fifty were killed, and eighty were taken prisoners and left to rot in Grey-friars churchyard until such time as they could be hanged or transported.

There are legends connecting the whole of the Pentlands, from Swanston to Dunsyre, with the Covenanters and the 'Killing Times.' Roger's Kirk, a rocky gorge near the western Black Hill, is said to have been one of their meeting-places; and the Wolf Craig, with its great mass of stone known as

Wolf Craig.

the pulpit rock, is reputedly another. Preachers like Cargill 'spoke a word' to the assembled people, and some who were leaders in the Pentland Rising may well have been amongst the hearers. Stern-faced men they were—certainly with much to make them so; not to be interfered with without some-times giving as good as they got. They brought other swords with them to their conventicles besides the sword of the spirit, and knew how to use them, as events proved.

What an extraordinary spectacle that must have been when, in the winter of 1681, a company of men and women with children, calling themselves 'the sweet singers of Borrowstounness,' left their homes and, chanting wailing psalms, climbed to the hills near the sources of the Leith Water, to witness from there the destruction by fire of the city of Edinburgh! One witness describes them as lying in 'the Deer Slunk in the midst of a great flow moss between Lothian and Tweeddale,' perhaps, like Jonah at Nineveh, in angry disappointment because the burning did not take place.

In 1745, by the aid of contemporary records, we catch a glimpse of the Young Pretender and his Highlanders coming south by way of Corstorphine, The keeping well out of the range of the Forty-Five. Castle guns. From the top of the Pentlands, through the eyes of the laird, or the tenant, of Woodhouselee—it is not very clear which—we can descry them in the distance, on the afternoon of Sunday, 15th September; and on the next day we can see the army of 'Highland Wifes,' as our informant sarcastically calls them, marching by the Braid Hills to the camp at Duddingston, while from 'Canaan Muir' we catch a glimpse of the young prince and his officers passing that way to Holyrood.

After the battle of Prestonpans the Highland army marched round the other side of the Pentlands to Milton Bridge on their way to Peebles. No doubt they were in high spirits—'All General Cop's wagons taken at Prestonpans' were with them.

During their stay in Edinburgh some of the Highland officers and men, who were quartered in
'Colington,' were in the habit of coming out to
what appear to have been open-air preachings held
at Dreghorn, by the Rev. Adam Gib, a leader of
the Anti-Burghers, and familiarly known as Pope
Gib. Mr Gib was a strong upholder of the existing
constituted authority, and his plain, denunciatory
speaking about the Popish Pretender must have been
anything but palatable to these Highland hearers.
The wonder is that he was not subjected to personal
violence.

Of the connection of Allan Ramsay, of the Fraser
Tytlers, of Lord Cockburn, of Stevenson, and others,
so much has been written, that here it is altogether
unnecessary to write more.

There is no great wealth of historical incident
connected with these homely hills. To the lover of
them their charm is a personal one. To tramp them
is a perpetual delight. Their outlines are varied.
Their colouring at all seasons is charming. Hill is
diversified with valley, cleuch and hope, loch and
stream. The views from their tops are interesting
and extensive, ranging northwards to Lochnagar, a
distance of seventy miles, and southwards to the
Cheviots, a distance of fifty miles. In the short
space of two hours a good walker from Edinburgh
may be alone with Nature, and feel the 'bliss of
solitude.' Of the rest and the tranquillity which
they impart to the tired spirit, of the invigoration
and the health which they bring to the jaded body,
one can speak only in superlatives. They are
stimulating, tonic, sedative. They are food and

medicine. Their air is intoxicating, and leaves no evil after-effects. Their charm is varied, all-prevailing, perennial. Alone with the hills one feels 'not far from the Kingdom of Heaven.' Breezes more fragrant by far than those of fabled Arcadia will play upon the cheek, and the ear will catch strains of that eternal music which is neither of earth nor of time.

THE PEAKS.

HILLS, like human beings, may be said to have personalities peculiarly their own. Some may be much alike in bulk, shape, and colour, just as in the case of men and women, but many of them undoubtedly present peculiarities in each of these characteristics, which distinguish them one from the other. While many of the south-western peaks are so softly rounded and lumpy in appearance as to be practically alike, there is considerable variety, in both outline and bulk, in the north-eastern peaks. The colours, at the varying seasons of the year, with a few exceptions, differ but slightly over the whole range.

The Pentlands, as has been already said, are but homely hills. They are 'kindly solemn hills,' to use Dr John Brown's words. They do not make *Peaks and Peculiarities.* any powerful appeal to the imagination by reason of their height or mass. To the rock-climber they offer practically no attractions; neither do they advance any great claim to the attention of the scientist. There is nothing uncommon about the birds or beasts that make them their home; nothing rare about the plants or flowers that nestle in their glens, or clothe their hill-sides; nothing very unusual to the ordinary observer about their geological formation. They are mainly for the hill-walker, the man of open heart and humble mind, who seeks no 'great things,' but finds his delight in the common sights and sounds of nature. They are for the man whose faith it is that the hills are better than the mountains, and who loves them with the child's love of its mother.

It is difficult to say which of them makes the strongest appeal to one, much depending on individual taste. Scald Law has height and mass, but is wanting in contour and colour. Of the many Black Hills—there are six altogether—the one best known, which strides across north and south from Threipmuir to Loganlee, and east and west from Den's Cleuch to the Green Cleuch, has great mass and lovely colour at all seasons of the year, but its outline is poor. Carnethy has height, mass, a beautifully-contoured outline, and, at certain seasons (though not to such an extent as Black Hill), very lovely colour. The West Kip, as seen from the east and west, has a beautiful outline, and is of a fair height, but it wants bulk, and there is not much heather on it. It is the graceful lady of the range. Most hill-walkers unhesitatingly vote for Carnethy as the finest peak.

In the brief notes which follow it has been deemed expedient to take the peaks in the order of locality, commencing with Caerketton at the north-eastern extremity, just behind Swanston, and ending with the lesser-known peaks at the south-western extremity.

Caerketton, though not one of the highest peaks, is certainly one of the most interesting. The best view of it is perhaps from about Hunter's Tryst, or between there and Hillend, and the best time of the year to view it is in late May or early June, when the blaeberry bushes are in the first flush of their new season's beauty. The soft colouring of the leaves, where the bushes

Caerketton and its Screes.

run along the tops of the rocks in wavy ribands and
festoons, or where clumps nestle in crevices, or zig-
zag across the screes, is a foil and a contrast to
the cold gray of the volcanic rocks.   Amongst the
winter snows the dark rocks also show to great
advantage, with their coping of white, and the long,
straight, steep slope descending from their base.

Caerketton and Allermuir from Comiston.

An impressive effect is produced during the occurrence of one of the little storms which are so common
with us during the spring months.   The rocky outline of the hill seen against a dark gray sky; the
heather and the screes powdered with snow; the
snowflakes pouring over the rocks, and blurring
their outlines; the mist trailing across the slope;
or the rain driven in sheets between one and the
hill—any of these makes a picture that remains
indelibly impressed on the memory.   The rocks
and the screes of Caerketton are amongst the finest
features of their kind in the whole Pentland range.

In 'Gellatly's New Map of the country twelve

miles round Edinburgh,' and in other old maps, this
hill is called Kirk Yetton. Readers of Stevenson
will not need to be reminded that he also applies
the same name to it. I have an idea that this
spelling of the name may have resulted from the
pronunciation of Caerketton by some old Scots
worthy. I have known similar mistakes made by
persons not thoroughly conversant with the Lowland
Scots tongue. Caerketton, I have no doubt, is the
old name. The map before referred to contains
various inaccuracies, and what one would reckon
nowadays as mis-spellings; and there are many
items omitted which ought to have been included.

McClure, in his *British Place Names*, states that
'*cett* appears in an early charter as tumulus.' 'We
have thus,' he says, 'in Caerketton the district of
the people who assembled at the *cett* or tumulus.'
Possibly the pile of wasted stones on the eastern
end of the ridge, which appears to be slightly the
highest point, is what now remains of the *cett* or
tumulus. Readers of Lord Cockburn's books will
recall that he reckoned Caerketton to be one of the
three finest view-points in Scotland, the other two
being Ben Lomond and Dumyat.

About a quarter of an hour's walk south-west of
Caerketton lies Allermuir Hill, from some view-
points one of the most shapely peaks of the Pentland range. Those writers who would
derive all our place-names from the Gaelic
have found their usual derivations of Allermuir.
Johnston gets it from *al-mor*, 'big rock,' and Milne
gets it from *ail airidh*, 'hill of the fold.' But one
is constrained to protest against this. As compared

Breezy
Allermuir.

with many of the other peaks, both in bulk and
height, Allermuir cannot be called big; neither can
it be said to be specially rocky; and it is hardly
fair to get quit of the word muir by transforming
it into mor. I think that, in the long flattish slopes
that almost surround the hill, we have the key to
the origin of the name. It is the hill of the aller
muir, *aller* being probably a corruption of alder.
The word is still so used in the south of Scotland.
Certainly no "allers" are there now, but evidently
trees have grown on these slopes in former times,
and the situation would be quite suitable for alders.
The view from the summit of Allermuir Hill is a
remarkably fine one, particularly towards the Loganlee glen and the noble range of hills beyond it. The
best way to approach the summit is by the high
path, above the Howden Glen, and across the western
shoulder of the hill. From this path the south-
western peaks, from Castlelaw to the Cairn Hills,
come gradually, one after another, into view. Allermuir Hill seems to me to be one of the breeziest of
the Pentland tops. I always have the feeling that
it is windier there than anywhere else. Possibly
this may be owing to the fact that, one stormy
afternoon on the summit, I had my hat whipped
off my head by the wind, and, after one momentary
vision of it in the distance, lost sight of it for ever-
more. Occasionally, when the wind is westerly, one
gets a whiff from the oil-works at Oakbank; and
sometimes, when the clouds were low, others besides
myself have fancied that they smelt the smoke of
Glasgow. In winter, when the wind is northerly,
it comes up the Howden Glen with great force; and

should light dry snow be lying, it is lifted and carried over the summit of Allermuir and down towards Boghall in driving masses like the waves and the spray of a storm-tossed sea.

In coming up the Howden Glen I have frequently had the wind strongly in my face up to a certain point, and then as strongly in my back beyond that point; or it might be the reverse.

Sir Archibald Geikie, in his *Scenery of Scotland*, says that the marks of the glacier ice can be seen on the top of this hill. Had he meant by this, the rounding and polishing of the rock surfaces, I could have testified to having seen these; but if, as I am led to believe, he refers to the striation and scratches which determine the course and direction of the glacier ice, I must say, doubtless from want of knowledge of the subject, that I am not so certain about these points.

Good views of Allermuir Hill are to be obtained from the northern slopes of Carnethy, or Turnhouse

Caerketton and Allermuir Hill from Fernielaw Avenue, Colinton.

Hill, and, perhaps best, from the upper slopes of Torphin Hill.

The rocks at the Green Craigs, which are situated at the foot of the Howden Glen, and a short distance to the south of the mansion-house and steading of Dreghorn, are interesting, although not of any great height. There is fine, warm, ruddy colour about them, especially when the westering sun strikes across their rugged surfaces and scree-covered slopes. I fancy that in these rocks we may find the origin of the name Dreghorn—*dearg*, red, and *horn*, a protuberance or projection. The greenness is not about the craigs themselves, but on their grass-covered summits. The so-called Reindeer Cave there appears to have been a dyke of some softer material intruded into the harder volcanic rock of the craigs, and now, worn away by the action of the elements, it forms a fissure rather than a cave. The finding of bones of various wild animals, including those of the reindeer, in this rock fissure, indicating it to have been the lair of some wild animal in early times, is fully described in the Pentland Guides and need not be more than referred to here.

At the south-western end of Torduff Reservoir there are also some rocks, which combine picturesque grouping with warm colouring, particularly in the autumn and winter months. The reservoir takes a fairly sharp bend there, and the rocks rise steeply out of it like a bluff headland. They are of a ruddy colour, and are festooned and banded with the rich orange of the withered brackens. The water, owing, it is said, to the presence in it of impurities—minute microscopical plants—appears always of a fine green colour, and on a calm day the reflections of sky and cloud, rock and bracken and tufted grass, produce wonderful colour-effects. To a certain type of imagination it seems the very spot for the enacting of a tragedy, where silently the suicide might leap into the green depths, or the murderer's victim might be hurled shrieking over the red rocks. At the foot of these rocks is a shallow cave, which is exposed to view most summers when the water in the reservoir is low.

Torphin Hill is a grass-covered, inconsiderable height on the northern outskirts of the Pentlands. There is no heather on it, but a good portion is covered with whin and bracken. The summit is the view-point from which Grecian Williams said that Edinburgh so much resembled Athens; but, as the hill is now laid out for a golf course, the enjoyment of this view by outsiders is not encouraged by the lessees. Torphin is, in all probability, the rock of Phin (or Finn), and attention has been called by some writers to the use of the same words in the name Corstorphine.

As a view-point Castlelaw (due south of Aller-muir) is one of the finest peaks—perhaps the very finest—in the whole Pentland range. From the summit cairn you look down on the Castlelaw. little lochs—real lochs, although they are popularly referred to as ponds—of Glencorse and Loganlee, with the gleaming rivulet twining down the glen, accompanied by the narrow white roadway. On one hand is the striking outline of the range of Turnhouse Hill, Carnethy, South Black Hill, Scald Law, and the two Kips, lit up with sunshine, or chequered in light and shade; on the other hand is

the great bulk of the Big Black Hill, almost sure to
be a mass of solemn shadow. Away beyond these
to the south-west, rising and falling 'like an earth
ocean moveless,' are the round-backed, lumpy hills
of Mount Maw, Spital Hill, Green Law, and Gap
Law, finishing with the finer outline of East Cairn
Hill with its bluff-like northern termination, at
whose base lies Harper Rig Reservoir. Nearer at
hand lie Threipmuir and Harlaw reservoirs, the
latter glinting through the trees which encircle it.
Farther away on the left hand are the hills between
Tweed and Yarrow, with the blue smoke of Peebles
drifting lazily across them ; the Moorfoot Hills, with
Portmore and Gladhouse reservoirs, like light streaks,
at their bases ; the Lammermuirs stretching away
eastwards towards the sea ; and all the fertile
Lothian lands which lie spread out in front of these
hill ranges. Through the gap where the Moorfoots
and the Lammermuirs seem to intersect towers up
the mass of the Cheviot, not very often visible,
however. On the right the Perthshire mountains
can occasionally be seen, with the nearer Ochils and
the Fife Lomonds—and on rare occasions some of
the Grampians—the fields of Fife and Midlothian
sloping down to the silver Forth, the silver of
which, too often, unfortunately, is dulled or altogether
hidden by the hanging heat haze or the gray wet
mist.

Castlelaw is a famous hill for viewing sunsets
from, especially during the winter, when the sun
sets far to the south, and so often irradiates the
glen and the surrounding hill-peaks. From the
Glencorse loch the eight-hundred feet climb of the

law is an excellent test of whether a man is sound in wind and limb. It is one of the best climbs to be obtained amongst the Pentlands.

On the southern slope of the hill is a considerable deep depression, which might be called a little corrie. There is not, as with the Highland corrie, the accompanying lochan, but I have no doubt there has been water at the foot of the slope in the distant past. Close beside the adjoining farm-steading there are the remains of a British camp or fort, the outline of which can, so far as it has not been destroyed, be very easily traced from the hill-top. There has been a double rampart and ditch, both of which are very perfect in places, on the side next the law, although they are somewhat effaced on the side next the farm-steading. In some parts the outer ditch is deep enough to hide a man standing upright. A relic of this old camp, and of its inhabitants, in the shape of a flint arrow-head, was found a few years ago at the summit cairn on the law.

The suffix *law* in this name takes us back to Saxon times, and more than probably, the prefix *castle* is derived from the old British entrenchment just referred to. Such old earthworks are frequently spoken of popularly in Lowland Scotland as castles.

I have somewhere seen the statement made that in old maps the names of Turnhouse Hill and Castle-law are transposed, but I have not been able to verify this statement.

Castlelaw is a fine massive shapely hill as viewed from the south-west, say from about the top of Glencorse Reservoir. A good view of it is also obtained from the opposite slopes of Turnhouse Hill, but perhaps the most imposing view is the one from the Glencorse Burn, immediately below the reservoir.

Castlelaw from the Glencorse Road.

There a portion of the top of the law appears suddenly over and through the trees. As thus seen at the early darkening of a winter day the little bit of blue hill looks far away and of unknown height, more a mountain than a hill.

The knoll to the north of Castlelaw is known as Fala Knowe; that to the east as Castle Knowe. The name *knowe* is said to be derived from, and to indicate the near presence of, the fort.

Woodhouselee Hill is the unimportant eminence to the east of Castlelaw. At its southern base are Allan Ramsay's bower and, a little more to the east, a small enclosed burying ground belonging to the Fraser Tytlers. A sunk path or ditch, partly encircling the hill, bears a strong resemblance to the well-known Catrail, which extends from the Cheviot Hills to Torwoodlee near Galashiels, and as to whose origin and use so much discussion has taken place.

The White Hill, so called from its being entirely covered with bents, which give it, during most parts of the year, a 'lintwhite' appearance, lies to the south-east of Bonaly House, the residence which Lord Cockburn erected for himself on his marriage in 1811. A few other White Hills, more to the south-west, are also indicated on the map.

One wonders as to the origin of the names of Cape-law and Harbour Hill, between which the most northerly right-of-way, the one from Colinton, descends to Glencorse. Bell's Hill, also named Belld Hill, and sometimes Beild Hill, is separated from Harbour Hill by the Maiden Cleuch, through which the second right-of-way, the one from Juniper Green and Currie, passes to its junction with the Colinton path on the hillside above Glencorse Reservoir. There is nothing specially distinctive about any of these three hills. There is some heather about every one of them, but they are all very largely grass covered. On the flat top of Capelaw small pieces of sandstone may be picked up from the bottoms of the drains. In some cases these are exactly similar to the yellow carboniferous sandstone which overlies the coal and the shale about Niddrie, Straiton, and Loanhead. In other cases they resemble the Old Red still found at the Cairn Hills. The glacier ice seems to have done its work thoroughly, and to have shorn away almost everything from the Pentland Hills that is of any value commercially.

To the south-west of Bell's Hill, and separated from it by Den's Cleuch, lies the most important of the The Big six hills which carry the name of Black. Black Hill. This is known as the Big Black Hill, the long, hog-backed mass so prominent in any view of the Pentlands from the north. In the 1811 Plan published by Creech, it is named The Logan House Black Hill.

It is the most massive of all the hills, but its outline is poor. It has no distinctly defined top. Like the Cheviot, though on a lesser scale, its summit is a long stretch of flat, wet, boggy tableland. Throughout the changing year there is richer colour on its steep declivities than can be found anywhere else on the whole hill range. In spring, summer, and early autumn the heather, tawny, dark green, or glowing purple, according to the season, contrasts with the bright green of the masses of wavy ferns that clothe the hill-slopes, and the brilliant green of the grass around the many little springs that filter out through the volcanic rocks. In late autumn, and during most of the winter, Black Hill is gloriously coloured. The great patches of heather, now a tawny brown,

Black Hill and Hare Hill from the North-west.

alternate with the orange of the withered brackens. The vivid green spots, even more brilliant than in summer, around the little springs and by the water courses, repose like oases amidst deserts of bleached and withered bents. Where the rock crops out and the screes trail away down the hillside there are warm ruddy streaks, and purple patches where the heather has been burned and the bare rocks show amongst the charred roots. Through and through the variegated pattern, in every direction, run the little paths which the sheep and the rabbits have made, cutting up the brown and the orange, the purple and the green, into the most intricate mosaic work.

A good view of these richly pictorial effects is obtained from the path between Currie and Glencorse, on the northern side; while an even better one is that on the southern side from the Kirk Road, the path from Loganlee to Penicuik, which climbs to a height of about 1500 feet on the *col* between Carnethy and Scald Law. To be there on the afternoon of a calm, sunshiny, winter day, when the rich colours of the hill are mirrored in the smooth waters at Loganlee, is to enjoy a vision of rare loveliness. The real lover of the hills is satisfied, and has little inclination to go farther afield in search of hill beauty amongst Swiss alps or Highland bens.

The rocks at the foot of this Black Hill, near the north-eastern end of Loganlee Reservoir, have occasionally some magnificent icicles, ten and twelve feet long, depending from them. When the sun shines on these long crystal spears they flash with the rarest of rainbow colours.

The name of Black Hill has, without doubt, been applied to all of the peaks so named on account of the generally dark colour which they present, owing to their being in the main heather covered, just as the grass and benty coverings have led to the naming of Green Law and the White Hills.

This Big Black Hill viewed from the north-east during the afternoon or evening seems to be always true to its name. While Turnhouse Hill, Carnethy, Scald Law, and the Kips may be more or less lit up by the sunlight, the Black Hill, owing, perhaps, partly to the angle at which it lies to the sun's course, is nearly always enveloped in a breadth of solemn shadow. Particularly in an evening light and as viewed from Allermuir Hill or Castlelaw the effect is very grand and impressive.

Geologists tell us that the rock forming the Black Hill is an 'intrusive igneous rock of Lower Old Red Sandstone age.' They say it is 'by far the best known intrusion in the Pentland Hills,' and consists 'of a somewhat dappled micro-granite or fesite,' which 'has intruded itself as a laccolite along the unconformable junction line between the Silurian and Lower Old Red Rocks.'

This completes the list of the hills on the northern side of the Loganlee glen and the Green Cleuch. We will therefore retrace our steps, and describe the peaks in their order on the southern side of the glen.

The first in order is Turnhouse Hill, a long, rambling, irregularly shaped hill, dipping down on its northern side into the waters of Glencorse Turnhouse Reservoir, sloping on its southern side into Hill and Rullion the high-lying district which stretches Green. away to the Moorfoot Hills, and forming on its eastern side the termination of the Pentland range. A portion of the north-eastern slope of Turnhouse Hill is, perhaps, the steepest part of the whole Pentlands.

Turnhouse, instead of gathering itself into one

massive peak, has frittered itself away, and wasted its substance in an effort to produce several peaks, not one of which has much appearance.

The name Turnhouse Hill looks an extremely modern one, but I have not been able to obtain any certain clue as to its origin. Possibly it is a corruption of some older name. Dr Milne, in *Place Names of Midlothian*, says that Turnhouse is corrupted from *Torr na Chuith*, 'hill of the fold.' But he seems by some means or other to get an extraordinary number of 'hills of the fold' or 'fold hills' amongst the Pentlands. For instance, Bell's Hill is 'fold hill,' Mealowther is 'head of the fold on a shieling.' Oxgangs is 'old fold.' He seems to have started with the fixed purpose of deriving all names from the Gaelic, and one gets, to say the least, a bit suspicious, when one finds him deriving *Radical Road* from *ruith a choill*, and Threshie Dean from two Gaelic words signifying 'heathery den,' a somewhat inappropriate name for a place where there is practically no heather, but an abundance of threshies or rushes.

The battle of Rullion Green, as mentioned elsewhere, was fought on the slopes of Turnhouse Hill, and at the edge of the wood on the southern slope of the hill, some four or five hundred yards from the Biggar Road, a memorial stone to commemorate the battle was erected by an unknown person in 1738, as the date on it shows. It is enclosed by a low parapet wall with an iron railing on top, erected about 1852 by the late Lord Inglis of Glencorse, at that time Lord President of the Court of Session. Recently a barbed wire fence has been interposed between the field and the wood, which makes it somewhat difficult to get near enough to the stone to read the quaintly spaced and worded inscriptions. These are as follows. On the face :

> *Here*
> *And near to*
> *this place lyes the*
> *Reverend Mr John Crookshanks*
> *and mr Andrew m'cormack*
> *ministers of the Gospel and*
> *about fifty other true coven*
> *anted presbyterians who were*
> *killed in this place in their own*
> *Inecent self defence and de*
> *fence of the covenanted*
> *work of Reformation By*
> *Thomas Dalziel of Bins*
> *upon the 28 of November*
> *1666   Rev 12-11   erected*
> *Sept 28 1738*

On the back :

> A cloud of Witnesses lyes here,
> Who for Christ's Interest did appear,
> For to Restore true Liberty
> Overturned then by tyranny.
> And by proud Prelats who did rage
> Against the Lord's own heritage.
> They sacrificed were for the laws
> Of Christ their king, his noble cause.
> These heroes fought with great renown
> By falling got the Martyrs crown.

A little to the west of this stone are the remains of another British encampment similar to the one at Castlelaw. The ditch is distinctly seen from the slopes of Turnhouse Hill. This camp has been cut in two by a field dyke, and the portion on the south side of the dyke has been obliterated.

The various peaks on the southern side of the Loganlee glen, composing what is known to frequenters of the Pentland Hills as 'the range,' are separated from one another by more or less considerable depressions, which form the summits of natural pathways from one side of the hills to the other, and are known as *cols*. To the south-west of the first *col* lies the peak of Carnethy, in the estimation of most hill lovers the finest peak in the whole Pentlands. Carnethy is only the second highest hill, but viewed from most points, owing to its peak-like shape, it looks quite the highest. It has a noble outline from any north-easterly view-point, sweeping up from Glencorse Reservoir in a long flowing curve, which steepens and stiffens as it approaches the summit, and then drops sharply down on the other side until it is lost behind the line of Turnhouse Hill. From the west and south-west the top has a peculiar dome-shaped appearance, as of the dome of a church springing from the intersection of the nave and transepts, the nave approaching towards the spectator, and the transepts spreading right and left. This is finely observed from the high ground above the waterfall beyond Loganlee Reservoir. Seen from Flotterstone, or Penicuik, or anywhere to the east, Carnethy looks magnificent, almost a Highland ben.

From Penicuik it is quite like Ben Lomond. A
very fine view of this grand hill is obtained from
the top of Den's Cleuch, where the mass of Carnethy
almost fills up the gap between the Big Black Hill
and Bell's Hill.

The steep slopes are strewn with screes, and the
summit is crowned with an immense pile of stones,
certainly a hundred tons of them, which looks in
the distance like a ruined castle. In early summer
the returning foliage of the blaeberries gives some
beautiful notes of colour amidst the cold gray of
the screes, especially when lit up by the fitful sunshine. In July there is a rich glow from the heath,
or ling, on the southern slope. Later the heather
purples great patches of it. In September, when
'infant frosts begin to bite,' glorious in their decay
as in their revival, the blaeberries blaze out again
in crimson and gold. In winter, ghostly and white
in the pale light of sunset, its base hidden in blue
haze, and its summit edged with purple or rose
colour, it looks abnormally lofty and far distant.
And so the whole round year rings the changes with
the beauty and the grandeur of Carnethy.

On the south-west spur of the hill, near the top,
an interesting section of the soil is laid bare, showing two to three feet of rich peat, the accumu-
lated withered bents and heather of many thousands
of summers, laid on the top of sand and gravel. In
winter the peat is soft, and a stick can be thrust
into it up to the handle, while in summer it is tough
enough to resist even a kick with the foot.

The huge pile of stones on the top of Carnethy
is not a natural feature. It is not the wastage of

the rock, but is undoubtedly the remains of some artificial structure. I am inclined to think that in this pile of stones we have the key to the name of the hill. The Gaelic word *Carneddi*, which means, 'the cairn of the heroes,' appears to be the same word as the hill name in its modern spelling of *Carnethy*, the *dd* in Gaelic having the same sound as the *th* in English. Almost certainly, then, this great pile of stones is a tumulus, the grave of some ancient British hero or strong man, or of a number of heroes.

Winter visitors to the hill-tops take both pride and pleasure, and often expend considerable energy, in restoring the cairns there, which, somehow or other, always seem to be falling down again.

On the *col* between Carnethy and Scald Law, the immediately adjoining hill, the Kirk Road between Balerno and Penicuik climbs to a height of almost

Scald Law. 1500 feet above sea-level, with fairly steep inclines from both sides. Scald Law, 1898 feet above sea-level, one mile (as the crow flies) south-west from Carnethy, is the highest peak of the whole Pentland range. It has considerable mass, but is somewhat deficient in outline. It is a truncated cone, with an acre or two of flat tableland on its top, and some wet boggy places on its south-western spur. Very evidently it has been severely glaciated. There is practically no outcrop of the underlying rock. Everywhere the hill has been smoothed and rounded, and, except for some trailing screes on its southern face, it is grass or heather covered all over, so that, saving in the months of August and September, when all the

hills are more or less resplendent in royal purple,
Scald Law has little or no colour except the soft
green or white of the bents and the darker or
lighter green of the heather foliage when the
flowering season is over. There are a few plants
of cloudberry near the summit.

Scald Law is, more than probably, Poet's Hill,
and is an example of the curious mixing of place
names which has often occurred when a district has
been occupied successively by different peoples. *Scald*
is from the Scandinavian, and means literally a
sounder or reciter, almost certainly a poet, while
law, as is well known, is an Anglo-Saxon word for
hill.

Mention may here be made of the rocks at the
head of the Loganlee valley, on the slope of Scald
Law, near the waterfall, an excellent place to observe
the wastage which is taking place through the action
of rain and frost. The large blocks of stone, which
have been broken away from the rocks and lie at
their base in confusion, there to be split into smaller
and ever smaller fragments, until they are finally
resolved into earth, are typical of what is going on,
in a greater or lesser degree, all the world over.
At the eastern end of these rocks a strong wooden
seat, with the words 'Peace, Perfect Peace' neatly
cut on it, has been fitted into a V-shaped recess in
the depths of which a foxglove nestles. It is not
known how long the seat has been there, nor who
fixed it in position. Perhaps it was some studious
person; perhaps some visionary. In any case the
site has been selected with care and judgment, and
the work has been well done. It is snugly sheltered

from the prevailing winds ; the view of hill and dale, wood and water, is a fair and pleasant one ; and, far removed from all jarring sounds, there, if anywhere, ought 'Peace, Perfect Peace' to be found.

The East Kip, sometimes also called the Little Kip from its lower height than the West Kip, is a somewhat featureless hill from most view-points, owing to its want of mass and to its south-west spur detracting from its peaky appearance. An exception to this, however, is the view from the top of Loganlee Reservoir, and from there all the way down the glen until the hill is lost sight of. The objectionable spur is not seen, and the outline is extremely graceful and imposing.

East Kip and West Kip.

The West Kip, as seen from the north-east or south-west, is a shapely conical hill, apparently tapering to a point. The view from a little distance up the Monk's Road shows this feature very finely. There is but one point from which it can be got ; a step or two in any direction from this point and it is lost—the perfect cone-like shape disappears. Observed from the north-west or the south-east, the top of the hill appears as a somewhat broken ridge. So sharply does it run up to a point that the ridge is in most places not more than a yard in width, and on a windy day there is difficulty in a walker's keeping his footing on it. Most hills have an appearance of strength, a masculine air ; but the West Kip is a lady, slender and graceful. It reminds me of some views of Schiehallion. By reason of its unique shape it can be easily distinguished from all the other hills. It stands alone, without any supporting buttress such as nearly every other hill has. I have seen and recognised it readily from such widely divergent hill-tops as Lammer Law, Blackhope Scar, Culter Fell, Tinto, Ben Ledi, and Ben Vorlich. I remember a very striking appearance it presented from Allermuir Hill one wild, stormy winter afternoon at sunset. There was a considerable amount of dry snow lying on the hills, which a boisterous wind was whirling before it. The sun was just disappearing, almost behind the Kip, when suddenly the whole sky in its neighbourhood was suffused with a most glowing yellow, upon which the graceful outline of the hill was drawn, with the snow whirling off its top like smoke, and ascending into the air in an apparent spiral. It looked like a 'burning mountain,' and recalled to me a picture, with which I used to be familiar in my school-boy days, of the Antarctic volcano Erebus in active eruption. It was clear hard frost at sunset, but by sunrise next morning the rain was descending in sheets.

The West Kip is, as has been said, of a graceful outline, but it wants mass. The blaeberry bushes enrich it with their soft spring colouring, and the heather glorifies it in autumn. It is, however, mostly covered with benty grass. The name *kip* is Anglo-Saxon for peak.

Turnhouse Hill, Carnethy, Scald Law, East Kip, and West Kip are ranged fairly well in line along the Loganlee valley, and form what may be called a miniature sierra. Due south from Scald Law is South Black Hill, like all the other Black Hills, well covered with heather. It presents quite an imposing appearance from the Biggar Road. On the top there

is a great pile of stones similar to what is found
on Carnethy. These heaps of stones, it may be
repeated, are not the wastage of the rock, neither
are they modern cairns which winter and rough
weather are hurrying to premature ruin and decay.

'The Range' from Kirk Burn.

Reading from left: Turnhouse Hill, Carnethy, Scald Law, East Kip,
West Kip.

Very evidently they are ancient erections, and the
presumption is that they are tumuli.

These are fine hills to walk over at any time of
the year. Only in a few places are they wet and
spongy in bad weather.

Hare Hill is the unimportant height stretching
from the Green Cleuch to the Logan or Kitchen
Burn. As already noted, the stone-heaps on the top
of this hill are not antiquities, but the debris from
a quarry which has been worked in comparatively
recent times.

The right-of-way from Balerno, known as the

Nine Mile Burn path, skirts the west side of Hare Hill, and passes on to the base of the West Kip, where it divides. The left-hand path goes down hill by Eastside to Silverburn, while the right-hand one skirts the edge of a wood, and after climbing to the summit of a *col*, runs down a valley on the other side, round the base of Braid Law, through a field to Nine Mile Burn Inn, and then by the old road to Carlops. This is one of the most interesting walks in the Pentlands. The views of the hills from it are remarkably fine.

Gap Law, Green Law, and Spital Hill are three very softly rounded hills, mostly grass covered and green, lying between the Nine Mile Burn path and the North Esk Reservoir. All are delightful hills to walk on in summer, although Green Law and Gap Law are apt to be wet in bad weather. Attention is called elsewhere to the existence of an ancient stone, and the numerous place-names, indicating the presence of monastic buildings in the near neighbourhood, during the Middle Ages.

Cock Rig, the height lying to the west of Green Law, introduces a new descriptive name into the nomenclature of the hills. The word rig is a corruption, or contraction, of ridge. There is nothing striking about the appearance of Cock Rig, although on its northern side there is a section showing the rock formation, which is worth looking at.

Two of the most interesting peaks of the whole range are the East and West Cairn Hills, between which passes the Cauld Stane Slap path through its solitary muirland surroundings, connecting the Lanark

Road at Little Vantage with the Biggar Road at West Linton. The East hill is the better seen of the two, and is a prominent object from all the peaks at the northern end of the range. One writer on the Pentlands says that it looks to him like a great snail. From certain view-points this is so, but from others it looks more like a great dog, a hound or a mastiff couchant and facing the wintry north, and I like to think of it as such. It seems to be always of a lovely colour—inclining to blue or purple, as if there were constantly a haze between it and the spectator. When approaching the hills from Balerno on a winter's day, and when nearing the muir at Bavelaw Castle, the walker should not miss the view of the East Cairn Hill through the trees there. As thus seen, the shadowed hill appears in patches of the most heavenly blue. When one reaches the muir and gets an unimpeded view, somehow or other the glory of the colouring is lost. It becomes only a gray colour inclining to blue or purple.

The Two Cairn Hills.

On the east side of the East Cairn Hill a wild-looking little hope, in which the Henshaw Burn winds its sinuous course, runs well into the shoulder of the hill. At the head of this hope, as a note in the Right of Way Society's Guide Book informs us, 'an Edinburgh W.S. named William Thomson, built a house in 1750.' On Gellatly's 1834 map the site of this building is laconically noted as Thomson's Wa's. I have carefully explored this place and can find no traces of a house, although there are the remains of walls which have evidently enclosed a portion of the muir. Within these walls the house

P.H.

may have stood, or these remains may represent
Thomson's Wa's.

Even to the most casual observer it is evident
that the rock formation of these two Cairn Hills
is different from that of the hills which we have
previously described. Geologists tell us that it is of
Upper Old Red Sandstone age, and where it crops
out, all over these hills, it is weathered in places into
very remarkable shapes, which look exactly like
architectural remains. Some of the stones are square,
some are circular, and others are angular of various
shapes. Time, with the wind and the rain, the frost
and the sun for chisels, has hewn them into these
shapes, and ornamented them with mouldings, the
very counterpart of those to be found in the remains
of our mediæval ecclesiastical buildings. There are
bases with the long sweeping ogee moulding, inter-
spersed with ovolos of most delicate and subtle
curvature, rounded beads, and hollows divided by
square fillets, arch stones with roll and wave mouldings, and deep undercut hollows, so difficult for
tradesmen to work, and bell-shaped capitals that
might have crowned tall, stately, clustered columns ;
not perfect by any means, but with parts broken off
here, and parts wasted there, as if the stone had
been subjected to rough usage in the one place, or
had been of softer texture in the other. Most of
the stones are of large size, and standing amidst
them one could almost imagine that some great,
glorious Gothic church, or abbey, had in the past
crowned the top of the hill. In other places the
rocks have weathered into shapes like gargoyles,
resembling the heads of prehistoric monsters. The

summit cairn on the East hill is an immense pile of stones, almost as large as the one on Carnethy. There is buried history in these stone-heaps, could one but know how to unearth it. This peak was long thought to be the highest of the range, but it has now been found to be only the fourth highest.

The summit of the West Cairn Hill is a long plateau almost a mile in length, and a rare place for

East and West Cairn Hills and Cauld Stane Slap.

a tramp. The cloudberry flourishes abundantly on this portion of the hills, more abundantly, I think, than on any other portion. At the extreme south-west, on a spur known as Colzium Hill, lie two boulders named the Ewe and Lamb.

A romantic place is Wolf Craig, fully a mile south-west from the cairn on West Cairn Hill. It is an outcrop of Old Red Sandstone rocks, lying at a slight angle on either side of a gorge, down which the Baddinsgill Burn tears its way angrily after heavy rains and spring thaws. The burn, however, is but young there, and in dry weather the gorge is little

more than a rugged burn bed. Most of the rocks
are on the north side of the gorge and present the
usual deeply and fantastically weathered appearance
common to this formation when it is exposed, some
of them looking like the great guns of a battleship.
On the south side an enormous mass of stone,
known as the Pulpit Rock, has been undermined, and
has partly broken away. It now lies detached from
its original position. All about the rugged rocks, in
nooks and crannies wherever it can gain a foothold,
the cloudberry nestles with its fairy-like flowers in
the June sunshine.

It is quite possible that the wolf may have had
its lair here in bygone times, or the name may have
arisen from the possibility of such having been the
case. One wonders if Scott borrowed the name and
transferred it to a different locality in his *Bride of
Lammermoor*. Stevenson might have woven it into
Weir of Hermiston, but Stevenson does not appear
to have known this part of the Pentlands. His
references, so far as my knowledge goes, are all to
the more northerly parts of the hills. Here, then,
is an opportunity for any budding novelist to weave
round this solitary spot, right in the heart of the
hills, some thrilling story. It would lend itself
admirably, from its name, its situation, and its
features, to some deed of daring, of cruelty, of love,
or of romance. I have the pleasantest recollections
of various *al fresco* meals, alone and in company,
amongst the rocks and cloudberries of Wolf Craig.
On one such occasion a member of our company,
seeing what he took to be a white hare somewhat
in a *cul de sac*, tried to run it down, more for fun

than anything else. The rest of us, interested spectators, wondered why the hare made no effort to escape; but just as it seemed on the point of capture it quietly hopped into a burrow. It was a pure white rabbit.

The hills more to the south-west are, as has already been said, somewhat featureless. There are few sharp bluffs or headlands; no outcropping rocks; no trailing screes, or 'sclidders,' as country people call them. Nearly all the slopes are long and flattish, and the highest peaks are only slightly higher than the lowest peaks to the north-east. Consequently they are not so interesting, but they are not without attractions of their own. They are for the most part somewhat unpleasant to walk over in winter. Owing to their flat slopes the rains and melting snows do not drain off quickly. In this respect they resemble certain parts of the Moorfoots, although they are not by any means so boggy as these. If any walker wants to know what the Moorfoots are like in this respect let him try to make his way in late autumn or early spring, not to mention winter, across the Rough Moss on the east side of Blackhope Scar. The Pentlands have nothing to offer in the way of long jumping that will stand comparison with the Rough Moss; in fact few hills have, so far as my experience goes.

But these south-western Pentlands are not always wet, even in winter. It is very pleasant to be on them on a frosty day, when the sun shines out of a clear blue sky, with a ring of haze all round the horizon, and possibly a foot or two of snow, frozen hard, covering the ground so that one can walk on it as on a pavement. The air is so exhilarating that, once one has reached the top of Dunsyre Hill, with a favourable wind one can almost run to the West Cairn Hill. In midsummer there is nothing more delightful than to be alone with the silences amongst these lumpy, homely hills. Even then the air is so cool and pleasant that I have walked from Dunsyre to Caerketton without losing a drop of perspiration.

The South-Western Hills.

The hill now named Wether Law is called Harper Rig on the 1834 map previously referred to. The name Harper Rig now designates the reservoir which lies at the northern entrance to the Cauld Stane Slap. There are some grand examples of rock weathered into the shapes of gargoyles on Wether Law. Seen from a little distance in a gray light they look quite fearsome.

Adjoining Wether Law and almost due south from it is Deerhope Rig, the first instance we have come across of the use of the word hope, which is so common amongst the Southern Uplands. It indicates a valley running into the hills and terminating there, having no outlet, in contrast to a cleuch, which is a through valley. These hopes are thus often spoken of as blind. Deerhope, without doubt, refers to the former presence amongst the hills of the wild animal whose name it bears.

The hill known as The Mount is shown on present-day maps almost between Wether Law and Deerhope Rig. On the 1834 map it appears considerably to the south of Deerhope Rig, almost in the position occupied by the hill now known as Mount Maw.

Mount Maw is a great lumpy, grass-covered hill, without any well-defined top. In summer it is green, and in winter it is mostly white. Except in Mount very dry weather, it is apt to be wet. Maw. The rain and the melting snow neither run off nor *seep* into it. I suspect there is a good layer of impervious boulder-clay between the grass and the underlying rock. It is said that there are both lead and silver in Mount Maw. Certainly

The Mount and Wether Law from Hare Hill.

there are evidences of mining operations having been carried on in bygone days. The name Lead Flats, applied to one of the lower spurs of Mount Maw, gives further weight to this, as does the name Lead Law applied to a height near West Linton. There is also a tradition in the village of Carlops that Cromwell took his soldiers up there to pay them, the narrator indicating 'up there' by a wave of his hand towards Mount Maw, a tradition which may be accepted, or rejected, at the option of the hearer.

The great mass of Mount Maw, under favourable atmospheric conditions, can be well seen from Castle-law or Allermuir Hill overlapping the West Kip and Scald Law. It is lower than these two hills, but is considerably more bulky. Next to the West Cairn Hill and White Craig Hill, which is a spur of it, Mount Maw is the highest ground—one cannot say peak—to the south-west of the Cauld Stane Slap.

Faw Mount is practically a continuation, at a lower level, of the slope of Mount Maw.

On the opposite side of the Lyne valley to Mount Maw and Faw Mount are King's Seat and Byrehope Mount. King's Seat is a common hill-name in Scotland. It occurs in the Ochils, the Sidlaws, the Lanarkshire Hills, near Biggar, and in other places.

Due west from Byrehope Mount, on the opposite side of the eastmost West Water (it is curious that there are two West Waters within about two miles of each other), are Fadden Hill and Craigengar. The latter name has a strong Gaelic flavour about it, and may mean rock, or hill, of the goats. Muckle Knock on Cairn Muir is evidently Scoto-Gaelic, although it is known locally as The Clock. On the summit of Craigengar are several stones with various names, but all having the surname of Dunlop, incised on them, with dates ranging from 1881 to 1909. Muckle Knock is a great grass-covered mound, its greenness being in fine contrast with the prevailing tawny colour of the muirland from which it rises. I have not been able to find any trace of a cave which is said to be on Craigengar.

South from Fadden Hill is Catstone Hill, the name of which undoubtedly indicates that it has been the site of some prehistoric battle. It is significant

that at the base of this hill there are two large
piles of stones, which are known locally as the
Battle Cairns. Through some oversight the name
of this hill has been omitted from some copies
of Bartholomew's large scale map of the Pentland
area.

West of Craigengar and Fadden Hill are Millstone
Rig and The Pike, both sloping down into the pastoral
valley of the Medwin Water, near its source. The
Pike is a featureless hill, but White Craig viewed
from the north-east resembles exactly the ugly snout
of the fish just named, and one wonders if the name
of Pike should not be applied to it.

About a mile to the north of The Pike is a hill
with the Gaelic-looking name of Mealowther, and
about another mile farther north is another hill with
the curious name of Torweaving—in Gellatly's 1834
map it is Torwoaving.

The long flat slopes of Black Law—or Black Hill
as Mr Reith says it ought to be called—rise on the
west side of the Medwin valley. This hill has a
The   mean-looking appearance, but is interest-
Covenanter's ing on account of the white stone stand-
Grave.   ing near its top, on the western side, and
marking the site of what is popularly known as
The Covenanter's Grave. The story is that this
Covenanter escaped wounded from the slaughter
at Rullion Green, and, dying somewhere in the
neighbourhood of Black Law, was buried in this
solitary spot. Standing beside this simple head-
stone, one can look through a gap in the Pentlands,
away into Ayrshire, and see the hills there, some
thirty miles distant, stretching across like a faint

blue rampart. The tradition that this man desired to be buried within sight of his Ayrshire hills may be quite true. Frankly, I accept unreservedly all that refers to the martyr's love of his native hills. I like to think of him as an idealist, with a strain of poetry, peeping like a wild flower in the cleft of a rock, out of his stern Scottish piety. Standing by his grave, I bare my head and consecrate his memory in my heart as a lover of the hills.

I have stood by the grave when the morning rays of a June sun were tempered by an easterly breeze; I have passed by that way when the white stone was hidden amongst the snow drifts of March; and I have reclined at length among the bents in the evening light of a glowing September day, when the view from the gravestone was a fair and pleasant one. Tinto and Culter Fell were all in deep shadow of a dark indigo colour. Between them Green Lowther rose faintly. Black Mount was in brilliant sunlight. The Tweed hills were wreathed and banded with thin wisps of mist, white as the clouds which floated slowly across the sun.

The inscription on the stone is as follows :

Sacred
To the Memory of
A Covenanter
who fought and was wounded at Rullion Green
November 28 1666
And who died at Oaken Bush the day after the battle
And was buried here
by
Adam Sanderson of Blackhill.

It is not quite clear whether Adam Sanderson was the man who succoured this poor Covenanter in his hour of need, and afterwards gave him decent burial, or whether, as is alleged, he was the person who removed the body from a hastily made grave in another locality, and re-interred it here, like that of Moses, on a hill-top. Surely there are none who visit this lonely grave but will invoke a blessing on the memory of Adam Sanderson, and sanctify a corner of their hearts to the nameless man who died for conscience' sake.

Mr Reith, in *The Breezy Pentlands,* says that this Covenanter's name has been ascertained to be John Carphin. He does not, however, quote his authority for this statement.

There are the usual stories and legends concerning the incident, but to what extent they are to be accepted as substantiated facts, or taken with reservation as purely traditional, it would be difficult at this distance of time to say. It appears, however, that the grave was opened in 1817, and the various articles unearthed indicated plainly the presence of human remains. An interesting account of what took place, and what was found in the grave, and also of the various traditions floating about the district, may be gleaned from an article contributed to the *Weekly Scotsman* of 7th December 1907, over the signature P. F. Dunlop, Dolphinton. In this article it is stated that 'it was at the instigation of Dr Manuel, Minister of Dunsyre, and mainly at his expense that the stone was set up about the year 1841.' The ruined house of Blackhill, of which Adam Sanderson was tenant, may be seen in the valley of the Medwin, about three quarters of a mile to the south-east.

Slightly over a mile south-west from the Covenanter's Grave is Bleak Law (which we are told should be Black Law), to the north of which is a series of heights, five in number, commencing with Wether Law, and terminating with Darlees Rig, running almost in a straight line from south-west to north-east. The heights are fairly equally spaced, and rise gradually from 1301 feet to 1462 feet above sea-level. The five elevations are as follows: 1301, 1347, 1361, 1376, 1462 feet. To the south of these is another eminence known as The Pike (1315 feet), and to the north is Harrows Law (1359 feet). There are shapely, well-built cairns on three of these heights.

To the north of Darlees Rig is Henshaw Hill (1299 feet). The first portion of this name is curious, and one wonders what is its meaning, and whence its derivation. It also occurs as Hen Hole for a deep rocky gorge running far up into the great shoulder of the Cheviot. Dr Milne says that *hen* in the Gaelic is hill. Henshaw is therefore 'hill of the wood.'

South from Bleak or Black Law are Mid Hill and Dunsyre Hill sloping down into the valley of the Medwin Water, a stream which is here of considerable size. Dunsyre Hill, although only a trifle over 1300 feet in height, presents from the east a most imposing appearance as seen in profile. On one occasion a party, including the writer, was approaching it from West Linton. It had rained in the early part of the day, and there was blue haze in the middle distance. Suddenly through the filmy screen a mountain loomed up large and precipitous, like a Highland ben. It was only some four miles away, but the haze made it look twice that distance. None of us had ever seen the same view of it before, and there was considerable speculation as to what *mountain* it could be. I believe there were visions of rock-climbing passing through the heads of some of the party.

The heights more to the south-west, although all over a thousand feet above sea-level, are little more than knobs rising from a score to a hundred feet above the surrounding muirland. The names of some of them are curious; as, for instance, Horse Law, Left Law, Lingy Knowe, Seat Hill, Yield Brae, Twin Laws, Shields Rig, Black Birn, Maiden Hill.

Mount Maw and Mendick from East Cairn Hill.

VIEWS—IN SUNSHINE AND STORM.

THOSE who are not in the habit of visiting the Pentlands have little idea of the expansive views which are to be obtained from this range. It is not, however, every day that these are to be secured. The atmospheric conditions must be favourable, otherwise one may go again and again and find his outlook narrowed in one, or it may be in all directions, either by haze or by mist. March is perhaps the best month for securing these wide views. If the sky is cloudy, without threatening rain, and the wind is blowing briskly out of the north-west, there is every probability of an almost entire absence of both haze and mist. Possibly about four in the afternoon the sun, which may have been hidden all day, will break in a fitful fashion through some rift in the cloud, and leaving all the nearer hills in solemn shadow, will cast a wan light on far-distant peaks which are still white with the winter's snows, making them stand out with vivid distinctness.

I do not concern myself with the views of the fair and fertile Lothians, of the Modern Athens, of the Forth—all these have had ample justice done to them. This is a book for hill-lovers, and I desire rather to draw attention to the many and far-distant hills and mountains which can be seen, under favourable conditions, from almost any of the Pentland tops.

The ranges of the Moorfoot and Lammermuir Hills

are usually, but not always, visible. The same may be said of the Fife Lomonds, the Ochils, such Perth-shire peaks as shapely Ben Vorlich, rugged Stuc a Chroin, Ben Ledi, the twin peaks of Ben More and Stobinian, Ben Lomond in Stirling-shire, The Cobbler in Argyleshire, and all the peaks that lie between and around them. On a rare occasion, such as has been described, the mass of the Cheviot, fifty miles away in a direct line, can be seen to the south-east through the gap between the Moorfoots and the Lammermuirs. On rarer occasions still a magnificent prospect, right into the heart of the Highlands, may be obtained, ranging from Ben More in far-away Mull to 'dark Lochnagar,' which frowns over Deeside, and is seventy miles distant from our view-point. Between tower the peaks of Cruachan overlooking the Pass of Brander, Ben Lui near Dalmally, Schiehallion in Rannoch, Ben Vrackie near romantic Killiecrankie, Ben Lawers by Loch Tay, and Ben y Gloe rising out of Glen Tilt, with many a lesser peak. Such a sight, however, may be had perhaps only once or twice in a twelve-month, and such opportunities are not only to be seized, but diligently sought for as a man may seek for hidden treasure.

Highland Giants.

From the south-westerly peaks glimpses may often be obtained away into Ayrshire, with the nearer hills of Tinto and Culter Fell in Lanarkshire looming up in front of them; behind these the Lowther Hills in Dumfriesshire; and, more to the east, to mention but a few, dark in shadow or dappled with sunlight, Broad Law, Dollar Law, and Dun Rig in Peeblesshire.

Not the least in interest are the views of the
Pentlands themselves from various points on them.
Reference has already been made to those from
Castlelaw, and such peaks as Carnethy, Scald Law,
and the Kips. Caerketton and Allermuir both afford
excellent stand-points, particularly at night-time in
winter. In front are the twinkling lights of the
city, and behind in silent majesty rises the group
of hills climbing out of the Loganlee glen, and
popularly known by hill-walkers as 'the range,' one
of the finest group of hills to be seen anywhere,
their beautiful outlines drawn clear against the sky ;
the outlook towards the city conjuring up a vision
of Man with his many interests, his unceasing
activities, his feverish restlessness, and the survey
towards the hills bespeaking the calm, majestic,
restful repose of Nature.

There are other things besides the desire to walk
and view the scenery which entice lovers of the hills
to the Pentlands. There are, for instance, the
wonderful sunset effects which can be seen from
them as they cannot be from the lowlands. As
Ruskin has said in the magnificent chapter in
Modern Painters which he calls 'The Mountain
Glory,' 'There is no effect of sky possible in the
lowlands which may not in equal perfection be seen
among the hills, but there are effects by tens of
thousands, for ever invisible and inconceivable to the
inhabitant of the plains, manifested among the hills
in the course of one day.' These effects are to be
seen at all seasons, but perhaps the atmospheric
conditions inducing them are most frequent during
the winter months.

Occasionally the tramper experiences almost wintry weather amongst the hills at midsummer. I recall one such day. It was the 5th of June by the calendar, but the weather conditions were those of November or February. My companion and I could not keep our hands warm even in our pockets. We had to descend to the low ground and take a sharp walk on the roads in a sheltered situation to restore warmth and animation to our limbs. There had been a blink of sunshine in the morning, but it did not last long. During the remainder of the day the whole sky was dark with lowering cloud, without a break in the mass. Between eight and nine in the evening, when we were coming down the Howden Glen, it became evident that there would be some unusual sunset effects. As the sun descended Sun and towards the horizon the all-prevailing Sky. mass became somewhat less massed, but, if anything, denser in texture. It was broken up into a number of cloudlets, leaving a clear space just above the horizon, through which the sun's rays shot down on to the far-distant country with a light which seemed a mixture of purple and gold. As the sun sank lower its rays shot farther out, and the magnificent glowing searchlight spread over a wider country, always advancing nearer us. From south to north there was a band of the purple golden light, stretching down in a great sheet, always spreading slowly towards us; touching the heights, the hills, the woods, the spires with glowing gold, and throwing the shadows into magnificent masses of indescribably rich purple. We stood, rapt in wonderment, waiting to be transfigured by the light. But it

failed to reach us. The sun dropped down behind
the Perthshire Hills, and the rich glow faded into
the gray of twilight. Above the sunken sun the
sky was palpitating with colour; red and gold,
yellow and green, blue and purple passing through
and into each other in a narrow space.

Here is the sunset of a soft November day,
during which a haze had enveloped everything.
The sunset is early at this season—about four

The Range from Howden Glen.

o'clock, even on the hills. As the sun dipped down
between the flat top of Mount Maw and the long
ridge of the East Cairn Hill the haze seemed all at
once to disperse to the horizon. In the neighbourhood of the sinking sun there appeared long fields
of blue and yellow, which towards the zenith shaded
into green, and towards the horizon shaded through
purple into red. Nearer the horizon were several
long narrow bands or bars of dark purple cloud,
between which the body of the sun showed of
a most brilliant crimson and of an apparently

enormous size.   Overhead were several thin clouds shot through with amber colour, drifting rapidly eastwards at a height that little more than cleared the summit of Castlelaw, on which I stood.   High above these were numerous cirrus clouds, quite motionless and pure white, their edges thinned away in the direction of the wind.   To the south the Moorfoot Hills loomed up faint and indistinct, while behind them towered great clouds looking like a range of snow-covered mountains far in the distance, mostly in shadow, but with magnificent peaks, here and there catching a faint purplish red glow, and reminding one vividly of climbers' descriptions of sunrises and sunsets amongst the Alps.   On the north Corstorphine Hill was faintly seen, behind which there were also clouds looking like a range of snow-covered mountains running from east to west with a long, nearly straight ridge of a uniform gray colour, except for a stripe along the top, which was of a cold clear white, ghostly-looking, and absolutely without colour.   In the east the Lammermuirs were completely blotted out, and their place taken by another bank of warm purple mountainous clouds, with a long undulating ridge-line, which was touched with a colour like flame.   This flame colour stopped abruptly at each end of the range.   The western Pentland peaks stood out as simple dark purple masses, the Loganlee Reservoir gleaming in the basin at their feet, with the silver ribbon of the little stream twining down the valley.   The effects so suddenly produced lasted but a minute or two, and then as suddenly faded away.

Here is a sunset under different conditions—those

of clear hard frost on a mid-December evening.
The hills were covered with snow, which was drifted
in places three feet deep. Climbing toilsomely up
the eastward slope of one of the peaks I was
rewarded, on gaining the top, by a sudden view of
a magnificent sunset. The sky was absolutely cloudless, but with a slight haze all round the horizon.
The sun was immediately above the haze, blazing
like molten gold, and everything in its neighbourhood, sky and hill-tops, was flooded with rich mellow
golden light, which shaded upwards through green
into a faint blue, and downwards over the hill-sides
into a most delicate pale purple, like a veil thrown
over the virgin snow. Round the horizon snow-clad
peaks were peeping up here and there through the
haze, each one touched with faint rosy light. As
the sun dropped into the haze—I fancied I could
see it sliding down—it gradually changed from
gold to dull flame, and streaks as of fire shot through
the haze along the hill-tops. The mellow gold and
the soft blue of the sky suddenly changed into a
pale cold gray—so cold and hard that the tenseness
of it might almost be felt, and the purple veil was
slowly withdrawn from the hill-sides, revealing the
wan features of the wintry landscape. The ruddy
gleam along the hill-tops, in the vicinity of the
sunken sun, lingered for a long time, and the haze
all round stood up like a dark wall or bank, with
Venus, the evening star, just above it, in the wake
of the sun 'glittering and throwing forth beams,' as
Richard Jefferies says, 'like metal consumed in
oxygen. . . .' In the evening hush, amidst the
gathering darkness, from the woods far below,

faintly through the thin air, the owls were hooting
eerily.

The last sunset I shall try to paint was one which
was witnessed on 10th August 1913. The sun sets
about eight o'clock, a little to the north of west, at
that time of year. In some respects this was one of
the most remarkable sunsets I have ever witnessed.
A party of four had been a fairly long tramp
across the hills, and were returning home over Castlelaw between seven and half-past seven. It was
too early for the sunset, but the evening was cold,
and we were thinly clad and could not wait, so we
continued to walk leisurely across to Allermuir Hill,
expecting to get a perfect view from there. All the
way across the colour was slowly increasing in richness, but even on Allermuir the perfect effects had
not been attained, so we kept moving on to Caerketton, casting many a careful look behind lest we
should miss anything. On Caerketton the feast of
colour was spread in all its grandeur, not very much
diffused, mainly concentrated in the north-west, but
of exceeding richness and beauty. The sun was
still a little distance above the horizon, and was of
a strong red colour, like a mass of heated metal, its
light softened by the evening haze, so that our eyes
could almost look on it unblinkingly. Upwards and
outwards the colour did not extend to any great
distance, but it was dazzlingly rich in crimsons, and
golds, and purples. From the Perthshire Ben Vorlich,
which was just peeping past the Ochils, to the
Dumbartonshire Ben Vorlich and The Cobbler, the
broken line of the Highland mountains cleft the
sky, while downwards, over their slopes, was spread

a warm luminous haze like dust of gold. The long
serrated mountain-ridge, fifty to sixty miles away,
appeared as one simple mass; grand by reason of
its simplicity; all its harshness softened, and all its
barrenness enriched and glorified by the wonderful
light shed over it from the sky. Every peak, great
and small, was softly defined against the rich golden
background, clothed in this marvellous raiment,
which now was like gold, and now like Tyrian
purple. Rising faintly out of the glorious palpitating light, in the far distance, were peaks which we
could not name; faint purple cones set in a sea of
gold. As the sun descended bars of cloud appeared
across his face, the dust of gold and Tyrian purple
on the mountains contracted in its area and paled
in its richness. The jagged lines of the peaks
bounded a sombre purple mass that was darkening
every minute. The sun's disc seemed to touch the
mountains. Immediately below it the gold and
purple reappeared, spread out within a narrow
circuit. Everywhere else the mountains rose in
purply-gray shadow. Slowly the sun descended
and went out of sight. The glow passed away
entirely from the mountain-slopes. The long broken
line from Vorlich to The Cobbler stood out more or
less distinctly, a solemn gray mass, against a sky that
was gradually changing from gold to crimson in its
light, and from purple to gray in its cloud-shadows.

Such sights as I have attempted to describe have
both a chastening and an elevating effect, making
one feel one's own littleness and meanness in presence
of the infinite richness and grandeur of nature, and
at the same time inducing a serene exaltation of

spirit, and a tranquillity of mind, which envelop one like a finer air.

Evening and morning are the principal times when the great painter 'flatters the mountain-tops with sovereign eye,' but the hill-walker sees many a sky-picture when the sun is westering, but long before it is near its setting. Sometimes, even when it is not beyond its meridian, there will be effects and colours which, were one to transfer them to paper or canvas, would startle the uninitiated.

Who that has experienced the joys of them can ever forget the April days amongst the hills, when 'the winter is over and gone, and the time of the singing of birds is come,' when sunshine alternates with shower, and towering billowy white clouds sweep across the far blue deeps of sky, the sunlight chasing the fleeing shadows over the wide open spaces like pursuing cavalry, and cloud following sunlight like the shadow of a god ? Or what tramper but remembers the wan sunlight of the winter's day ; the haze shot through, and made luminous by it with orange and purple light, moving as the vapour moves across the sun ; great beams of light slipping through openings in the clouds ; white silvery light, clear and cold as if coming from Sirius or the North Star ; swiftly moving light-beams, spreading out fan-shaped, touching here a hill and there a wood, glistening on the snow, gleaming on the waters, appearing and disappearing as suddenly and swiftly as the lightning's flash ?

Most persons look partly amused and partly sceptical when mention is made of night-walking on the hills. They are disposed to magnify the dangers,

which are really no dangers at all when there is a
moon.   A winter night is the best time for viewing
By Pale
Moonlight. the hills by moonlight.   It is, of course,
advisable to have a companion, and if
the weather is cold means should be taken to protect the body by the wearing of an additional shirt
or vest.   A cloudy night gives the most wonderful
effects, and if it is breezy as well as cloudy, with
the moon 'as if her head she bowed, stooping through
a fleecy cloud,' the beautiful effects will be greatly
enhanced.

It is surprising how far distant objects are distinctly visible at full moon in a clear sky, while
with a lesser moon every object, unless it is quite
close at hand, looks weird and ghostly; and the
alternate light and shadow, as the clouds cover or
clear off the moon's disc, the sudden fading or
brightening of the light concealing or revealing the
hills, produce effects which mere words are totally
inadequate to describe.

If snow has been drifted and lies in patches, and
the moonlight is not too strong, the effect is very
curious.   The snowdrifts assume faint shadowy
shapes which one cannot persuade oneself are not
masses of white vapour slowly encircling the hills.
Time and again I have fancied I saw them moving
towards me, and it was only with difficulty that I
could persuade myself that such was not the case.
The waters of the loch down in the glen gleam like
polished silver, and when the moon is in a certain
position she throws a faint yellow reflection from
shore to shore, in which the slightest ripple on the
water is seen.

If the enthusiast who goes for a walk on the hills in the moonlight is looked on somewhat critically, what is to be said of him when he spends the whole night there that from them he may witness the sunrise? This is well worth doing, however. It should, of course, be done during the summer or early autumn months, for the sake of warmth. Even then it is astonishing how cold the weather will sometimes be, while the heavy dew which occasionally falls not only makes the grass and the heather so wet that it soaks through the strongest boots, but seeps through one's clothes even to the skin. And after all one may not see much, for the glories of the sunrise are shy and elusive. Perhaps the sky may stir with flush upon flush of warm rosy light, passing from 'misty pearl to opal with heart of flame, and from opal to gleaming sapphire,' but more often the dawn comes not with observation. The darkness thins almost imperceptibly. There is a light gleam along the horizon, and faint tinges of rose and purple in the eastern sky. Or clouds may gather suddenly, massing and thickening in the direction of the sunrise, with long straggling mistbands hanging low on the hills all round the horizon, covering the hill-tops or drifting lazily across their green sides, like immense silver airships. Slowly and stealthily the dawn creeps up the sky, and spreads over the hills. For at least an hour its coming can be noticed, and yet no one can tell whence or how it comes, so gentle, so gradual, is its approach. The muir birds call plaintively. The whaups and the peesweeps seem scarcely to have slept. There is a rustle as of the earth shaking out her draperies, and the cool winds of dawn softly caress one's cheeks.

The sun is the great colourist in nature. There is no artist that can approach his chromatic effects. But the sun is not the only artist. The haze and the mist often produce wonderful effects. Mist-Pictures. They are artists in monochrome. While the sun paints with a full palette, the mist gets its effects with simple pen or pencil, or gray washes; and what a range of effects it can produce, from the wet raw fogs of November to the dry haze of June or July! Sometimes summer and autumn mists will lie so low in calm weather that by ascending a few hundred feet one will rise above them into an area of blue sky and cloudless sunshine, and from this vantage-ground will look down 'upon a world unknown, on nothing we can call our own.'

Here is a mist-picture as seen from the top of Allermuir on a July evening at sunset. From this point one looked down upon the cloud, which was then some hundreds of feet lower than the hill-top, as upon an immense snowfield. It gave one some idea of what Arctic or Antarctic scenery might be like. In the east, to windward, the range of the Lammermuirs was thinly white-veiled, and, their bases being hidden, the hills seemed unusually lofty. A little to the northwards, in the far distance, a small portion of the Firth could be discerned, looking like a peaceful inland lake. Nearer at hand the mist stretched from the base of the Pentlands right across to the shore of Fife, which appeared as a dark band of indigo shaded off on both edges, except at the western end, where the Ochils towered up

very sharply defined, and of a colour approaching
almost to ultramarine. On the west the mist seemed
to terminate between the Black Hill and the East
Cairn Hill. To the south the whole of the inter-
vening country between the Pentlands and the
Moorfoots was blotted out, and the Moorfoots were
also submerged. Thin white wisps of vapour were
creeping up the Loganlee glen and the lateral glens
to the north of it, but did not appear to be making
much progress there. They seemed to be dissipated
towards the head of the Loganlee glen, and were
floating about in long ribands and feathery-looking
patches. In the main the mist looked as flat as a
floor, although in places, especially near the Fife
coast, it was tossed into mounds, and peaks, and spires,
which caught the rosy light from the setting sun,
or it was furrowed into glens in which the shadows
lay dark. The tops of the Pentlands were all clear,
and the dark green of the heather, and the tenderer
green of the blaeberry-bushes stood out strongly
against the snowy-looking background. Occasionally a whaup sailed across on motionless pinions, or
a peesweep went by, its wings flapping heavily, or
some swifts careered madly after insects. All of
them were sharply defined against the whiteness.
Overhead, the blue of the sky was barely hidden by
soft filmy gray clouds edged with warm colour, with,
here and there, bright streaks of amber and rose-
pink; and in the north-west one point of glowing
crimson, where the sun was dipping into the haze
which shrouded the Perthshire mountains.

Summer mists are often strictly local; and I have
many a time noticed, when nearing the outskirts of

such a bank, that a smart wind will spring up, bringing with it great drops of rain. Sometimes the rain has been so heavy that I have felt impelled to run a hundred yards or so into the bright sunshine which I saw in front of me.

On days when there is little or no wind the movements of the mist are interesting. It will crawl over the hills and muirs, fanning gently at times like

Threipmuir.

the wings of a hawk poised in the air, and at other times stretching out long skeleton-like claws, as if it were some sluggish creature feeling for its prey.

The glorious chromatic sunset and sunrise effects, and the no less wonderful monochromes produced by the mist, are intermittent phenomena of nature.

Nightfall. There is another phenomenon of daily occurrence, less noticed, but none the less worthy of observation, the ending of the day, when the kindly, solemn, brooding night, 'the Shadow of the Eternal,' settles slowly and deliberately over the hills. The soft falling of the night amongst the hills is at all seasons peculiarly impressive. Perhaps one might say that in summer the nightfall is more beautiful, while in winter it is more solemn. The long summer gloaming, the soft, subtle, indefinable changes, the rich mellow haze effects, the opulence of nature, are full of beauty, and combine to soothe, to subdue, to intoxicate the imagination, as the subtle perfumes of the East soothe and intoxicate the brain. In winter the darkness is deeper. It gathers and fills up the valleys more quickly. The outlines of the hills are drawn hard and sharp against the clear pale gray of the sky. There is no blending, no softening of the edges, no running of one colour into another. While the darkness is gathering, and until everything is shrouded in the universal pall, the hills, the woods, the waters stand out as simple masses, impressive and solemn by reason of their simplicity. Hill-walkers who have been a whole day amongst the hills seldom care to go home without witnessing, from some vantage-ground, the glories of the sunset, or if there is no visible sunset, then the soft falling of the night; and he must be a dull fellow indeed in whom the nightfall does not excite poetic fancies.

Richard Jefferies somewhere remarks that it is never so dark in the country as it is in the town. This is true. In the country the darkness is diffused; in the town it is concentrated into the shadows cast by the street lamps. On returning home at nightfall after a day in the country it is only when the sphere of the street lamps is reached that one realises that it is really dark.

During hard frosty weather a curious sound is sometimes heard on the hill-tops, which, for want of a better name, I am in the habit of calling the hush

of evening, although it occurs at other times of the
day as well as in the evening. Blackmore alludes
The to it in *Lorna Doone* (Chapter XLV.).
Hush of With his keen eye and ear for natural
Evening. sights and sounds nothing seems to have
escaped his observation. 'One leading feature of that
long cold,' he says, 'and a thing remarked by everyone
(however unobservant), had been the hollow moaning
sound ever present in the air, morning, noon, and
night-time, and especially at night, whether any
wind were stirring, or whether it were a perfect
calm.' I remember hearing this sound very distinctly
one calm, frosty, Christmas night. A friend and I
had walked some twenty odd miles over the hills,
and we were nearing home. Just as we breasted the
top of Castlelaw the moon shot up in the east,
yellow and almost full. In the west the sun was
dipping towards the horizon, descending into a sea
of gold amidst islets of purple cloud. It had been
brilliant sunshine all day, but frost had never been
absent. As the sun set it got keener, and soon it
was freezing hard. It was a perfectly still, windless
evening, with this soft, subdued murmur coming
from everywhere and from nowhere. What is this
soft, hushed sound that one hears on frosty evenings
from hill-tops? One may hear the cawing of the
rooks as they settle down for the night; sounds of
human voices softened by distance; the faint bark-
ing of a dog; the bleat of a sheep—but these are
separate and distinct from the hush of evening. It
is an undertone, steady, soft, and low; like the rush
of water over a cauld; like the sound of trees sway-
ing in the wind. What is it? What causes it? It

is not the wind soughing through the withered bents,
for there is no wind. It seems to come from far-off
hills, from distant places, from the sea—a soft,
monotonous, soothing sound. Is it the wind retreating to the far-distant horizon? One cannot tell.
It filled the men and women of old time, as it fills
one now, with poetic fancies. Overhead the frosty
sky is hard and pitiless, but the hush of evening, up
there, alone with the stars, soothes and enfolds one like
the arms of the all-sustaining Mother. One feels that
it is good to be there, for the place is holy ground.

Another phenomenon, which it is interesting to
observe, is the action of the miniature spring or
summer storms, hail, or snow, or rain, according to
Wayward the season, which are so common in this
Storms. country. While travelling up or down
either a Highland glen or a Lowland valley, I have
frequently observed, in an adjacent or a branch glen,
one of these little storms travelling with or against
me. The long streaks of hail or rain, passing slowly
or swiftly according to the wind-current, appear to
drop and rise alternately, pursuing a long undulating movement—sometimes like the motions of an
immense horse, sometimes like the gliding of a huge
serpent, and at other times like the evolutions of a
great body of men in the air. From the top of
a hill occasionally quite a number of these little
storm-centres can be seen at once, travelling at
various distances, at different levels, and with varying degrees of velocity. It is interesting, too, to
watch how the different wind-currents act upon the
little storm-clouds. Sometimes one of them will
travel a considerable distance in a perfectly straight

line, streaming down towards the earth, and being
lost to view where it seems to touch the horizon.
Suddenly a current will catch it, and whirl it up,
or send it driving down at a great rate. At other
times a cloud may be deflected to one hand or the
other, almost at right angles, or it may curve round
in a sweep, longer or shorter, and then shoot away
in a straight line. The Pentland tops are excellent
view-points from which to observe the action of
these little storms.

From the vantage-ground of a Pentland peak
grand picturesque effects may be observed in
February or March, when the muirs are being
burned. Far and wide the smoke is seen rising,
trailing away for miles to windward if there is a
wind, or ascending in spirals to a great height if it
is calm. The smoke is thick and white. When
seen from a short distance it is tinted with brown
and yellow, where a sudden sunbeam strikes it, and
shaded with blue. Great tongues of ruddy flame
burst through the smoke here and there, twisting
and curling sometimes far above it, when the
conquering fire attacks a clump of whin bushes in
the line of its march. The ruddy glow through the
darkness of the night, as the fire eats its way along
a hill-side or runs along a hill-top, is a scene of lurid
grandeur. Round the edge of the 'burning fiery
furnace' various figures may occasionally be seen,
fantastically distorted, poking amongst the flames
with long poles, controlling the spread of the fire,
but looking in the distance somewhat demoniacal, as
if they were preventing the escape of 'puir damned
bodies' from Gehenna.

FAUNA.

WHILE there is nothing very outstanding to be recorded regarding the flora and fauna of the Pentlands—no rare beasts, birds, or plants to be noted as having their habitat there exclusively—there are, nevertheless, many interesting things worth mentioning regarding the life which is to be found on and around them during the varying seasons of the year.

MAMMALS.

Occasionally a fox may be encountered. I have heard his bark several times as I was returning home in the early darkening of a winter's evening. Master Reynard. I have also seen the prints of his feet in the snow, where he had crossed the tops of some of the hills. It is a clean, clear-cut print like that of a somewhat small dog. Once I met him full in the face. I had toiled up the Howden Glen, through an extraordinary April snowfall, to the summit of Allermuir Hill, and just as I approached the gate there from the west, reynard approached, a few yards distant, from the east. He was a fine large dog-fox, in beautiful fur, but very wet and bedraggled by the snow, and evidently much exhausted, as his tongue was hanging out a long way. I am, perhaps, as little of a sporting man (so called) as any man living, but I got over that gate in double quick time, with a whoop and a flourish of my stick. I fear reynard summed me

up as a fraud at first sight. He treated me with
silent contempt. He noticed me—and that was all.
Slightly altering his course and almost imperceptibly
increasing his pace, he cantered away downhill
towards Boghall. I have subsequently seen him at
various places on the hills. On one occasion I had
a close sight of him as he lay sunning himself in
front of his den near the summit of East Cairn Hill.
It is wonderful how accurately he can judge when
he will be out of sight of an onlooker. I have
observed that, just as he reaches this point, but not
before, he will give one look over his shoulder.

The blue, or white, or mountain hare, as it is
variously called, is met with mostly to the south-
west of the Cauld Stane Slap. It is only rarely seen
Hares and to the north-east of this path, although
Rabbits. it is certainly increasing in numbers on
the north-eastern hills. The fur is of a bluish tint
in summer, and pure white in winter. Its winter
whiteness is presumably protective, but as often as
not it is the reverse. Some winters little or no
snow falls upon the hills, and during most winters
there are longer or shorter periods of open weather,
when the snow is completely cleared off. At such
times a white hare is a very conspicuous object, and
can be seen from a long distance. When the fur is
changing from white to blue, the creature is as
beautifully marked as a Persian kitten. When
disturbed the white hare invariably makes for the
top of the hill, and the sportsman takes advantage
of his knowledge of this. A party of beaters is sent
along each side of a hill, while the shooters keep
a little behind them on the top, and the simple

creatures easily fall a prey to the guns as they rush instinctively for the summit. Another name by which this animal is known is perhaps a more appropriate one, that of Arctic hare. It is an immigrant to the Pentlands from lands farther north, where snow lies longer and more continuously and where its white fur is really protective.

The common or brown hare, while not to be found in any great numbers, is more plentiful at the north-eastern end than its white cousin, but, like the mountain hare, it is found in far greater abundance on the south-western hills and in the fields abutting on them. The brown hare is a much more alert creature than the white one.

Rabbits, contrariwise, seem to be most abundant on the north-eastern hills. On certain portions they are kept down remorselessly, and are scarcely to be seen. In addition to the ordinary gray rabbits, there are occasionally a number of pure black and a few pure white specimens, with many intermediate varieties, some of them with pure black faces and gray fur otherwise, and others of a grimy colour all over, like coalmen. These used to be quite plentiful about the Green Craigs at the foot of the Howden Glen. Some which I have seen there were almost as ruddy as the red earth amongst which they lived. The black varieties—possibly the white ones too— I presume, are freaks, or sports, just as black lambs are. Burrows are not very deep, and a great many rabbits must occasionally be crowded into them. Sometimes in muggy weather, when the hills are covered with snow, a steam may be seen rising from the burrows. The rabbits do not care about coming

out when such conditions prevail. In long-continued
frosty weather they suffer severely, and it is pitiful
to witness the efforts which they make to scrape
away the snow so as to get a mouthful of moss or
herbage. Some of the warrens are very thickly
populated, and are so situated that a walker comes
upon, and has time to observe, them before the
rabbits are aware of his presence. These warrens
always remind me of quiet country villages through
which I have passed on sunny summer evenings.
The rabbits, sitting round the mouths of their holes,
look just like old country people after the toils of
the day are over smoking a peaceful pipe, pottering
about their gardens, or enjoying the cool air or the
softened glow of the evening, while tiny tots, like
children, play about the doors.

Weasels and stoats are somewhat intermittent in
their local habitations. Occasionally one or other
of them will be seen at the same place for weeks
in succession. Then it will disappear, and
Weasels.
another one, or possibly the same creature,
will appear in another situation. On certain portions
of the hills which are patrolled by keepers neither
weasel nor stoat will ever be seen, incessant warfare
being waged against them. On one occasion I was
witness to an intensely interesting game of tactics
between a weasel and a starling. The starling was
perched on the top of a dry-stone dyke, and the
weasel was trying to stalk it from below, but the
starling, although a young bird in its first year's
plumage, was too wide awake. It was wonderful
to witness the cunning with which the weasel
endeavoured to climb the low wall unobserved,

taking cover under every projection, and worming
its way from one side of the wall to the other as
its stealthy advance was detected by the wary bird.
The wall on which this manœuvring took place runs
downward from a square angle at the top of Allermuir Hill, so that, standing on the top of the hill,
I was able to witness all the moves in the game by
simply bending my head a little to right or left.
What might have been the outcome of the strategy
I cannot tell, for the bird, happening to notice one
of my movements, took flight, and the wily little
tactician went his way downhill in search of fresh
adventures.

On another occasion a friend and I were just in
time to prevent a fine cock-pheasant falling a prey
to a stoat. We were passing toward a slap in an
old stone wall when we observed the stoat, a large
and handsome one, rush away, evidencing by its
ruffled fur its great anger at being disturbed. We
started in hot haste after it, for my friend had not
previously seen a stoat, and, scrambling over the
loose stones of the slapped wall, I almost set my
foot on the pheasant, which had been dozing or
sunning itself.

When a weasel or a stoat is hot-foot on the trail
of its prey it sometimes seems to get oblivious to
everything else. It will pass within a few feet of
an observer, or almost blunder up against him. I
have seen a weasel take to the water, and swim
across a burn quite as readily as a rat would do.
The tramper is continually coming across the silent
witnesses to the grim tragedies of the hills, a
constantly recurring one being that of the dead

body of a rabbit with the weasel's tell-tale hole in the back of its neck.

Squirrels are not generally to be found amongst hills unless there are woods on them, but I once encountered one near the Cauld Stane Slap, far from any wood. It was in the end of July, and the little creature was in beautiful fur of a very rich colour.

Rats may sometimes be seen, but always, so far as my experience goes, in the neighbourhood of human habitations. Water-voles frequent various burns.

Several varieties of mice make the hills their permanent dwelling-place, and their holes and runs may be seen amongst the bents—their runs occasion- ally under the snow—sometimes very prominently. The shrews, with their long snouts and their beautiful silky fur, I have frequently noticed about the West Kip. The little red-backed meadow-mouse I have also met far from meadows. Once after a heavy fall of snow one of these pretty little creatures behaved in a very diverting fashion. It was exploring about the roots of an old hedge, quite regardless of my presence, diving down into holes in the snow, and every time it came out of one of these sitting so jauntily on its haunches, and rubbing the snow off its nose with its fore-feet. Its track over the snow was like delicate chain-work. I recollect picking up the dead body of an infant field-mouse when passing to the hills one day. It was a tiny mite; something less than an inch in length, without fur, but with everything else about it perfect; the little legs, and the feet with their morsels of toes; the head, somewhat large

Mice and Moles.

in proportion to the body, with its blind eyes, its small tufts of ears, its slit of a mouth (about the thirty-second part of an inch in width and firmly closed), its specks of nostrils; everything in miniature, but everything complete. I fancied that its mother might have been shifting it from one place to another, when cruel fate, in the shape of some bird or beast of prey, overtook her, leaving the poor little thing to die of starvation. Without doubt, Nature is 'red in tooth and claw.'

Allermuir Hill from Kirk Burn.

The earthworks thrown up by 'the little gentleman in velvet' are to be met with in nearly all the valleys and lower slopes of the hills, although a war of extermination is persistently kept up against him. Occasionally fifty or a hundred corpses may be found, sometimes without the fur, sometimes with it, festering and polluting the air until beneficent Nature ultimately absorbs them. It is seldom one meets with a mole above ground. I have only three or four times had the experience, the first time in the Howden Glen. The meeting seemed to be quite a surprise to both of us, and 'the little gentleman' was evidently anything but 'pleased to meet' me. He rushed precipitately for a hole, but apparently it was not the entrance to his fortress. He stuck in the hole, his hind-legs frantically clawing the air. With some difficulty he extricated himself and rushed to another hole. This time he made no mistake, quickly disappearing under ground.

Two of my friends on one occasion found the dead body of what they took to be a pine marten on the Pentlands. When I saw it there were only the tail and a few mangled bones remaining, and I had not sufficient knowledge of this animal to pass an opinion as to its identity. It might have been a pine marten escaped from captivity.

The hedgehog is occasionally to be met with. In the twilight of a summer or autumn evening it may be seen scuttling away to its hiding-place. Oftener, however, it is found lying dead. It seems to be in a state of chronic outlawry, the hands of most men and boys and the teeth of all dogs being against it.

I am informed on unimpeachable authority that there are a few roe-deer on the hills. It has never been my good fortune to get a sight of any of these.

These are, so far as my observation goes, all the mammals to be met with on the Pentlands at the present time. Wilder animals, without doubt, did once inhabit them. The deer and the wolf have left their names to witness to their presence in bygone times, and their bones, found in the rock cleft in the Green Craig, confirm what the hill-names tell us. Several years ago an otter was found by a keeper in

the pool at the Loganlee waterfall. Unfortunately
it was accidentally killed.

BIRDS.

Amongst birds which frequent the Pentlands the
place of honour must, of course, be given to the red
grouse, which is not only born in the purple, but
spends its life (mostly a short one) and
Grouse. ends its days there. Every frequenter of
the hills is familiar with its strange cry, ending so
like the command 'go back, go back, go back.' I
have heard of an old lady who vocalised some of the
grouse calls to this effect: 'Lang Jenny; lang Jenny;
lang Jenny! I 'm comin'; I 'm comin'; I 'm comin!
Be quick; be quick; be quick!' In April, when they
begin to be very lively, the love-speeches of the male
bird sound, at a little distance, exactly like garrulous
talking. When the birds are paired, if they are
flushed from amongst the heather it will be noticed
that they always rise one after the other, and a few
yards apart. They are never quite together.

Amongst other curious things connected with the
red grouse the writer has to record the finding of
a newly laid egg, lying in a slightly hollowed stone
on the top of Caerketton, on the 17th of October.
The egg was smaller in size, and in shape more
tapering, than a normal grouse egg. The ground
colour was almost a pure white, and the mottlings
were correspondingly faint. When blown, it was
found to be perfectly fresh.

With the nesting of these birds the walker dates the
beginning of his troubles on the hills for the summer.
He is watched and hunted as if he were a dangerous

criminal. It seems strange that the presence of these beautiful birds, and the desire on the part of a privileged few to shoot them, should be thought sufficient reason for the exclusion, to such an extent, of walkers from so many of our Scottish hills. When on the nest the grouse sits very closely, and every man worthy of the name—certainly every hill-walker I have known—is anxious, as far as in him lies, to avoid disturbing the bird.

The young are able to run about almost immediately they are hatched. They are quaint, interesting little creatures, like chickens, covered with yellow down, and, when flushed, with infantile cheeps, quickly scatter to cover. The efforts of the parent bird, when thus disturbed, to distract the attention of the intruder from her young—pretending to be unable to run or fly—are very interesting, and have often been remarked upon.

No visitor to the hills can fail to notice the fact, which is continually thrust upon his observation, of the great wastage of life amongst the creatures which frequent them. Bird and beast have not only the gun of the sportsman, the snare of the fowler, the tooth and the claw of the assassins amongst their own kind, but also the elements of Nature to contend with. On a stormy afternoon in March some years ago, as I was approaching the top of Caerketton from the south side, a small covey of grouse rose in front of me. One of the birds seemed to be quite overmastered by the wind. It could not get the use of its wings, and was whirled along at an amazing speed, just clearing the heather, until it was dashed with such violence against a wire fence that it was instantly killed. It was a cock bird, perhaps a year old, in splendid condition, and in most beautiful plumage.

The red grouse is exclusively a bird of the hills. The black grouse, or blackcock, prefers field or meadow-land alternating with hills. It is very scarce on the Pentlands. I have never seen more than one blackcock at a time. On one occasion, however, I saw one cock and three hens in company. The pheasant is not a bird of the hills, but it sometimes visits them. The partridge is oftener found there. Woodcock occasionally belie their name by being encountered far from woods, pursuing their devious way when startled from amongst the bents or brackens.

On a spring evening, sometimes after dark, the curious bleating of the snipe may be heard in the neighbourhood of wet, boggy ground. It is a very peculiar sound, somewhat like the bleating of a goat, and there is a difference of opinion as to how it is produced. Some observers contend for the wings as the active agency, while others affirm that it is the tail. One afternoon in early May, as a friend and I were crossing the muir from Glencorse to the Howden Glen, we heard two snipes bleating, and located them wheeling about high overhead, certainly several hundred feet up. We watched them through a field-glass, and noted very carefully that the bleating was invariably heard when a bird was diving down with outspread, almost motionless wings and fan-shaped tail slightly curved in towards the body. I should not be surprised if both wings and tail have a share in the production of the sound.

The jack-snipe is a rare winter visitor to some parts of the hills.

With the advent of March the lapwings, green plovers, or peesweeps spread upwards from the fields to the hills. At that season their plaintive wailing note has a certain stridency about it, a tone of anger, well-nigh of menace, as they keep whirling round any intruder on their preserves, and almost smiting him with their wings. Some years ago there was a voluminous and somewhat animated discussion in *The Scotsman* as to whether the crest of the peesweep is green or black. From close observation of several dead birds found on the hills, I have no hesitation in saying that it is black.

The Lapwing's Wail.

The peesweeps are quickly followed, sometimes preceded, by the curlews, or whaups, which have wintered at the seaside. Every hill-walker keeps his ears open for the first note of the whaup. One friend of the writer's refers to it annually in this way, 'I heard it on Saturday.' It is peculiarly *the* summer sound of the hills—one of the grandest natural sounds. It is of the hills hilly, if one may so say. There is a wonderful glamour about it. It is like old Scottish psalm music : soft, melodious, long drawn out—like Coleshill or Martyrdom, as one has heard these sung in old country churches long ago. The whaups are extremely wary birds, and it is very difficult to discover their nests, but I have occasionally found them with their four big handsome eggs—once on the summit of Caerketton. This bird was very shy at first, but ultimately allowed me to come quite near to it, until at last

I was permitted to stand beside it as it sat on the nest. I am happy to be able to say that the eggs were hatched and the young birds seemed to get away from it in safety. Hill birds all sit very close on their nests, particularly when the time for the young birds hatching out draws near.

Following the whaups, also from the seaside, come the golden plovers. At times these birds seem to return to some of the hills even earlier than the whaups. I have heard them on the Pentlands, occasionally, as early as the middle of February, but as a rule (at this north-eastern end at least) they follow the whaups. The golden plover has two distinct call-notes. Its spring call Mr Abel Chapman describes as *tir-pēē-yŏu*. To me it sounds more like *oh-dēē-ar*. At other times it has a single, clear, flute-like note, which Mr Howard Saunders renders as *tlüi*. The dunlins are regular summer visitors to parts of the hills.

Kestrels may be seen most of the year, hovering over the uplands, mouse-hunting. I once met one full in the face, coming round the rocks on Caer-

Kestrels and Owls. ketton. It was greatly surprised, and pulled up sharply to avoid me. The wind was in its back, and it had some difficulty in turning round, so it shot straight up into the air. I could see both its wings and its feet going with great rapidity. It looked like a man hurriedly mounting a ladder. The sparrow-hawk is sometimes to be seen round the outskirts, but it is not much on the hills. The merlin's nesting-place is amongst the heather. I have found one at the Garvel Syke. It contained five eggs, four of which

were so closely covered with minute red spots as to
warrant one calling them red eggs. The fifth was
entirely different, being covered with much larger
spots, beautifully rayed. The merlin is an active
and daring bird, but one objects to the number of
small birds it kills.

That handsome bird, the common buzzard, I was
long in meeting on the Pentlands. I suspected its
presence, and in the end came upon it quite unawares.
A strange bird rose from the side of Threipmuir
Loch, and, flying low and heavily, settled on one of
the fences to the west of the road. There was
something unusual about its movements, and the
other birds seemed curious, excited, and hostile
regarding it. So my companion and I, getting the
bole of a tree in line with ourselves and it, carefully
stalked the bird to within about a dozen yards.
Immediately, however, we put our heads past the
tree it took flight in its slow, heavy, laboured way ;
whereupon there arose a perfectly deafening clamour
from perhaps two hundred sea-gulls, nearly all of
which tried to buffet the stranger, while it continued
on its stodgy way, evidently not caring much, until
it gained the shelter of a thick wood about a quarter
of a mile distant—an illuminating example of how
to behave when attacked by popular clamour !

The cry of the barn or screech owl once heard
is not easily forgotten. One is often startled of an
evening by its weird call from some of the old
buildings adjacent to the hills. The brown or
tawny owl hoots in the woods all the year round
as soon as the darkness begins to fall. Its cry is
the ' tu whit, tu whoo ' of Shakespeare, or, as John

Burroughs has phrased it, 'oho ho that I had never never been born.' It has sometimes flitted noiselessly across my path as I have been coming off the hills at nightfall, and, once or twice, on clear moonlight nights I have got quite close to one sitting blinking on the top of a dyke, and I have also seen a pair of them chasing each other amongst the fir-tree tops.

From May to at least the end of June the call of the cuckoo is constant amongst the hills, and the bird may be seen often at close quarters by any observant person. Dreghorn is one of its favourite and early haunts. It was once my privilege to see a young cuckoo being fed by its foster-parent, in this case a wagtail, amongst the screes on Caerketton. Without controversy it was a sweated industry. On another occasion, by hiding behind a tree in the T-wood at Swanston, I was enabled to keep two adult cuckoos under observation for a considerable time. It was 'in the leafy month of June,' and one of the birds was following the other through the intricacies of the wood, uttering the while a sound such as I had not heard before from a cuckoo—a curious bubbling sound, something like what a boy can produce by blowing into water through a tube. This bubbling sound is a call-note of the female bird. Heard near at hand, the two-fold note of the male bird is, as Wordsworth describes it, 'a hollow note.' It sounds more like hoo-hoo than cuckoo. The change in the tune of the cuckoo does not always wait for leafy June, as the old rhyme would make us believe. I have distinctly noticed the change in May. The variants were

' cuck-cuck-oo,' ' cu-cuck-oo,' and ' cu-hoo-oo.'   They
gave one the feeling that the bird was a stammerer.

The rooks are about the hills most of the year,
and doubtless pick up many unconsidered trifles.
They are not over particular as to what they eat,
and there are always dead creatures, from sheep to
mice, lying about.   One Christmas day, tramping
on the Pentlands with two friends, I found a very
handsome rook caught by the toe in a steel trap.
What a pleasure it was to set the prisoner free !   I
don't think I ever saw a bird fly so fast in my life.
It waited not 'upon the order of its going,' but
went like the wind, looking neither to the right
nor to the left, until it faded from our sight.

Jackdaws are often to be seen and heard amongst
the flocks of rooks.   The hooded crows are always
in pairs.   The *huidies* are not favourites with the
keeper, and get short shrift whenever met.   They
are too fond of grouse eggs, of which they are
notorious and expert thieves.   When on the hunt
for these delicacies they will work a hill-side in the
most scientific, systematic manner.   The handsome
plumaged carrion-crow is also a Pentland bird.

The raven is said not to frequent the Pentlands,
but I have on more than one occasion seen a pair,
sometimes three, of them, and heard their solemn
croak as they sailed slowly overhead.

The chattering magpie, with its beautiful shape
and equally beautiful plumage and flight, is to be
met with at various places where there are woods.
Occasionally one will be found impaled, with a nail
through its beak, against a tree or a wall, for what
reason one cannot exactly say, but presumably as

a sacrifice to grouse. The law which permits the rich man and his keeper to do this, and prohibits the poor man from taking, for a pet, any one of our lesser singing-birds, which are more plentiful than the magpie, can hardly be called an equitable law. The prohibition should apply equally all round.

The heron, perhaps the noblest of our wild birds, frequents the hills most seasons of the year. In summer one or two may generally be seen about the old burn courses which the shrinkage The Stately Heron. of the water discloses in the reservoir at Threipmuir. He haunts the Howden Glen too, and in the early darkening of a winter evening I have disturbed him at his solitary fishing, quite near to Edinburgh, where the little footbridge crosses the Braid Burn near Comiston. It is a fine sight to see, with the aid of a strong glass, the heron at his fishing. How stately he looks as he stalks about in the shallow pool or stream! Each foot is curled up as the leg is lifted out of the water. Slowly and deliberately the foot is replaced, and with unerring, lightning-like swiftness and force the long sinuous neck and the strong bill are shot out. He is a successful fisher. He hooks something every cast. The heron does not appear to breed about the hills. Perhaps the reason may be that there are no suitable nesting-trees. Since the foregoing was written a young heron has been seen in one of the Pentland glens, so that possibly an occasional brood may be reared on, or near, the hills.

A sea-bird somewhat akin to the heron, the

cormorant, occasionally visits Threipmuir. I have
recognised it there in the company of ducks. I
have also seen at Threipmuir what I took to be
barnacle geese.

A notable sight in winter is a flock of wild geese
passing over the hills, high overhead, in their usual
V-shaped formation, one side of the V sometimes
Wild Geese very much longer than the other. I have
and Duck. seen the difference as great as five on the
short side to fifty on the long one. The V, or
wedge shape, tapers to a point—one bird ; and the
birds are continually changing their positions, reliev-
ing one another. Their wings move as one, and as
they pass overhead, if one listens, one may hear their
call of ' Honk ; honk-honk ; honk !' like the ' Left ;
right-left ; right !' of the drill-sergeant to his recruits.
The lines of the V are occasionally straight ; but for
the most part, the longer line in particular, they
undulate in beautiful wavy curves, every bird keeping exactly its relative position to the bird in front
of it.

The common gull, the herring gull, and the black-
headed gull are regular visitants to the hills. In
winter and spring they are assiduous in their attend-
ance on the ploughman in the fields adjoining, and in
autumn they steal the farmer's corn. The lesser
black-backed gull is fairly plentiful, but the ' great '
variety of the species I have not often seen. Occasionally it rides at anchor on Glencorse loch. It is
well named ' great,' being the largest, by six or eight
inches, of the gull family, and a truly majestic bird.
Unfortunately its reputation is not good. It is
not only voracious, but a notorious freebooter into

the bargain. Along with the rooks, the gulls act the part of scavengers upon the hills, devouring all sorts of dead creatures. A bird akin to the gull, the common tern, has been observed, but not by the present writer, fishing in Loganlee Reservoir. I have, however, seen a pair of Sandwich terns at the same place. These have wonderful wing motion and are very expert fishers. Dropping from a height of twenty feet or so, they hardly ripple the surface of the water as they lift their prey out of it.

In February 1918 a flock, numbering between a dozen and a score, of fork-tailed petrels flew overhead as I was crossing the Nine Mile Burn path. They were flying eastwards in loose formation, and appeared to be migrating. There is no previous record, so far as I can find, of this bird having been seen about the Pentlands.

Persistently noisy birds during spring and summer, in the neighbourhood of water or damp ground, are the red-shanks, with their sharp *reishlin* call-notes. Fiona Macleod speaks of the red-shank's call as a ' windy whimper.'

The common or mallard duck is very plentiful about Harlaw and Threipmuir, and, in a lesser degree, about all the other reservoirs. It is a pretty sight to see a duck take to the water, with about a dozen ducklings in her wake, like a ship towing a flotilla of little boats. Teal ducks also frequent both Harlaw and Threipmuir. With the aid of a glass such occasional visitors, keeping well out from the land, as golden-eye, scoter, widgeon, tufted duck, and pochard, may be noted. Once, when I was climbing Caerketton, a number of widgeon flew

low across the screes, the sunlight glistening on their
beautiful breasts.

The coot, with its strange look and strange call,
is very plentiful on Threipmuir, and so is the water-
hen, while the sandpiper, with his ringing, startled
cry, is a summer visitor to Glencorse, Threipmuir,
and possibly the other reservoirs.

The wood-pigeon is not a bird of the hills, but it
may often be seen winging its rapid, easy flight

Harlaw Reservoir and West Kip.

across them. The blue rock-pigeon is a regular
summer visitor. I have found its nest at various
places.

Lying about the hill-tops on a warm July day
I have often heard the occasional twittering of the
swallows, or the screaming of the swifts, as they
circled round and round in pursuit of insects. Sometimes they have come so near me that I have heard
the swish of their wings, and felt the vibration of the
air on my cheek. I wonder if the air feels as sweet
to them as it does to me !

The house-martin and the sand-martin cannot, in any sense, be called hill birds, but I have seen them there occasionally.

On the Logan Burn, the little stream between Loganlee and Glencorse reservoirs, one will never fail, at any season of the year, to see the dipper winding its devious course, following every turn and bend of the stream; settling on a stone occasionally; becking and bowing, always keeping a little in advance of the walker until a certain point, the extremity of its feeding-ground, is reached, and then invariably turning and going in the opposite direction, or plunging into the water after the grub on which it feeds. He sings a merry little song, sometimes, from his cold perch on a frosty winter's day. This little bird bears a remarkable number of names in addition to that of dipper. An alternative one in the text-books is water-ousel. In some parts of the north it is known as the 'burn becker'; on the Borders it is termed the 'waitter craw'; while, according to Richard Jefferies, in the south of England it is the 'water-colley.'

Great flocks of starlings frequent the hills during the summer, as alert and wide-eyed and business-like as they are to be found in the fields or in the back-greens of the city. No doubt they are attracted there by the enormous number of insects which, at certain times, literally cover the grass.

Fieldfares in considerable numbers, with here and there a red-wing, also feed on the hills, particularly Turnhouse Hill, in winter. These are, however, oftener found on the lower adjacent grounds, especially if there is a wood near at hand to which they can retire on being disturbed. Starlings and missel-thrushes are sometimes in their company.

Missel-thrushes mostly frequent the uplands when fields and woods are in the neighbourhood, although one may be met with occasionally right in the heart of the hills. In some districts the fieldfare and the missel-thrush are known as the hill birds.

The song-thrush frequents the glens most of the year, and in his singing season, spring and early summer, if one is on any of the adjacent hill-tops about sundown, one will be sure to hear his clarion call floating up from the valley of Glencorse, or The Winter Loganlee, or from the so-called T-wood. Singers. The blackbird also frequents the glens, but in the good weather he goes farther up in the hills, sometimes to the very tops. In this connection I recall a most extraordinary burst of song, early in the season, to which it was my privilege to listen. On 25th March 1910 four of us took the early morning train to Dunsyre, and from there walked over the Pentlands to Edinburgh. About seven in the evening we were at the waterfall in Glencorse valley. The air was soft and phenomenally warm for a March evening. It seemed to act as a stimulant to the birds. Such a chorus I do not think I have ever heard equalled. All the master-singers were there, and all were in their best voices—wild whistling mavises, mellow fluting blackbirds, robin-redbreasts; with many lesser singers—hedge accentors, chaffinches, and greenfinches—whose notes we could hear between the pauses of the louder singers. At half-past seven, as we rested in our climb up Castlelaw, when it was quite dark, we could still hear the chorus coming up grandly from the glen, while two larks soared, one on each side of us, and sang for a brief space; and for half-an-hour afterwards we heard the bleating of a snipe as it wheeled over the muir.

The ring-ousel, which is the blackbird with a white ring or bib partly round its neck (more pronounced in the male than in the female), is a summer visitor to the hills. In some districts it is known as the mountain blackbird. Its nest I have found in various places on the Pentlands.

The true home of the skylark is the wilderness, the muirs that skirt the bases of the hills. Its song, which the slightest blink of early sunshine may call forth, is a lure and a stimulus to the hill-climber. 'Up with me! Up with me! Into the clouds!' he sings. Early spring and late autumn walkers amongst the hills have the song of the lark for their marching music; and in the sleep of winter the walker has his imagination stirred by the sight of the great open spaces, the benty grass, the heather, the blue sky, and the recollection of the lark's song like a waterfall there.

Among common birds which frequent the hills, and occasionally nest on them, are the sparrow, sometimes in immense flocks if there are fields of grain near at hand; the chaffinch, with its strong bold notes and its artistic nest, wherever there are suitable trees or hedges; robin-redbreast, with his poet's song in summer, singing from the trees in the glens, and nesting in the wayside banks. In company with one or other of these may be found the hedge accentor with its modest little song.

Flocks of greenfinches, with their contented, twittering notes, may always be met with; and that handsome bird the bullfinch has not quite left the hills. In winter the linnet also visits the whinny slopes and the adjacent roads in fair-sized flocks, and wretched men with trap-cages and bird-lime go out to snare them.

The yellow yorling is a fairly constant resident, especially in the neighbourhood of the roads in the glens. The wren, with its rollicking song, and its rather awkward movements—like a sailor ashore —a little man with a big voice, lurks about bushes and whins and by the burn-sides.

The three varieties of wagtail (pied, gray, and yellow), with their beautifully undulating greyhound-like movement and their sweet notes, may all be seen, in their season, in the Loganlee glen, and doubtless at other places where there is running water. The so-called white wagtail—a rare variety—I have observed there once or twice.

Those sharp little birds, the tits, particularly the cole tit, the great tit, and the little blue tit, are Tits and always in the near neighbourhood of the Chats. hills, if not actually on them, in woods and about farmyards. The long-tailed tit has been seen at the shooting-ranges at Malleny.

Our smallest native bird, the gold-crest, frequents the fir woods and the whins which fringe the road by the side of Glencorse Reservoir. It always seems quite indifferent to my presence

Amongst the pipits, two varieties, the meadow pipit in particular, like an abridged edition of the skylark, and, to a smaller extent, the tree-pipit (a migrant, this latter), are almost sure to be both seen and heard.

Of purely summer visitors one cannot fail to note, in the vicinity of rabbit burrows and old walls, the wheat-ear flirting its wings and displaying its white rump.

A shyer and rarer bird is the redstart. I have but twice seen it, once in the neighbourhood of Dreghorn, and the second time at Harlaw. The two chats, the whinchat and the stonechat—both very handsome birds—are usually to be found on the face of the slope between Swanston and Dreghorn. The stonechat, by the way, appears sometimes to stay all the winter there. The sedge-warbler, with its garrulous song, is an intermittent visitor where grass and rushes overhang the streams in the glens. So also is the reed-warbler, or, as it is alternatively called, the blackcap warbler. I knew it in my school-boy days as the 'coal heid.'

The willow-wren and the whitethroat coquette with the hills rather than pay serious court to them; they dance round their skirts. Separated by the breadth of the road from the hill-slopes, the song of the corn-bunting, redolent of the clod, may often be heard during the summer.

One of the most interesting birds to observe is the tree-creeper, as it works its way, spiral fashion, up the bole of a tree, in pursuit of insects and larvæ. I have seen this bird at work among the beeches at Bavelaw, and in the plantations at Woodhouselee.

Among purely winter visitors the snow-bunting, or snowflake, comes to the hills from the far north in a wonderful variety of plumage. A very rare visitor, so far as my observation goes, is the brambling.

A beautiful and interesting little bird I should like to see oftener is the siskin. I have had that privilege but once, in the Howden Glen.

That mystery bird, the corncrake, often heard but seldom visible, I have caught sight of in the neighbourhood of the hills. It walked quite leisurely in front of me as I was approaching the waterman's cottage at Torduff Reservoir, where the road passes through a cutting, and dived amongst the tangled herbage which covered the slope. I could plainly trace its course up to the field fence. There it seemed to come to a standstill. I flushed it, when it made excellent flight away past Bonaly.

There are other birds which are said to be frequent and steady visitors to the hills, and a few which are said to be regular winter visitors; but these have not come under my personal observation, although I have been amongst the hills at all seasons and in all weathers. No notice is therefore taken of them in these notes.

Many of our common butterflies spend their short lives among the heather. The whites and yellows are sometimes in great abundance. The red admiral, the two tortoise-shells (often), and the peacock (occasionally) spread out their wings there to catch the sunshine. From end to end of the hills the small heath may be seen fluttering during the height of summer; it must be in millions. The so-called common blue butterfly dances, like a bit of the sky, in the little hope down which the Kirk Burn bickers on its way to Glencorse

Butterflies.

Reservoir. They are in considerable numbers, and
when the westering sun throws a shadow across the
bottom of the hope, they fold their wings and go
to sleep upon the rushes. I know of no prettier
sight than that of those sleeping beauties. When
they are in. this state they will allow one to do
anything with them, except press their wings apart.
The beautiful emperor moth (almost like a small bird)
and two varieties of the gaudy tiger moth display
their colours in the summer sunshine. The more
sober-coloured fox moth is somewhat restricted in its
range, although it is to be found in considerable
numbers in the places which it does frequent. One
Edinburgh May holiday I found the burnet moths
in scores on the top of the West Cairn Hill. It is
wonderful how many of these creatures which we
look upon as having purely a summer existence are
to be found amongst the withered bents in winter—
flies, moths and butterflies of various kinds, with
even a *hairy-oobit* travelling post-haste over the
snow

FLORA.

OF plants which are to be found on the hills first place must, of course, be given to the heather, on account of its abundance, the wonderful beauty of its colouring, and the associations connected with it. Much of it is somewhat stunted and short in its growth. The finest plants for cutting are to be found on the lower lying grounds, preferably in the neighbourhood of trees. Some good specimens may be gathered every season on Currie Muir near Bavelaw. When the purple fades as the flowers wither a fine russet colour takes its place, which gradually deepens into the tawny brown of winter as the flowers drop off. The white variety is fairly abundant, much more so than most people think. I have gathered sprays of the genuine article from such widely different localities as Castlelaw, the Big Black Hill, and the Cairn Hills, but it was always in small quantities. It was never like the patch, as large as the top of a good-sized table, which I found several years ago on the summit of the Peat Law facing the town of Selkirk. It is a singularly beautiful sight to see a spray or two of white heather

Heather, Purple and White. amongst a great expanse of the common purple variety. It looks like miniature lily of the valley, or like a small spot of snow. The foliage is of a lighter green than that of the purple variety. The glory of the flowering heather is, without doubt, the attraction which draws so many visitors to the hills in August.

The heath, or ling, with its larger and somewhat

deeper purple flower, is both an earlier and a later
arrival than the heather, coming first in July and
reappearing in September after the heather has
faded. Although flourishing at considerable altitudes,
the ling is a fragile flower, and will not stand pulling.
It droops and fades in a very short time. Its
distribution is much more restricted than that of
the heather. It is, in fact, somewhat local in its
distribution. There is a good deal of it about the
Big Black Hill. If the tramper casts his eye upward
on his left-hand side as he comes down the Green
Cleuch towards Loganlee, the glow of the ling, in its
season, amongst the long screes and the ruddy earth
will greet his eye, while as he descends the steep
Kirk Road to Penicuik he will see it purpling all
the southern slope of Carnethy. Both the common
and the cross-leaved varieties are found in these
situations.

Ruskin has said, in *Modern Painters*, that Alpine
scenery is loveliest in April, whereas he finds that
most people prefer to go and view it in August.
Much the same might be said of our own Pentlands.
Most visitors are fascinated with the purple glow of
the heather, and the glamour which song and story
have woven around it, and think that August is the
right, the only, time for visiting the hills. This is
a mistaken notion. They are just as beautiful—to
me they are more beautiful—when the blaeberries
begin to expand their foliage, which may be in
April, May, or June, according to the season. There
is then a wonderful wealth and variety of soft
colouring, composing a beautiful mosaic, in which
there are patches of short grass of a bright emerald

green; great spaces of soft sage green, where the young grass is springing up amongst the white of last year's withered bents; streaks and patches, and in some cases great masses, of blaeberries of a brilliant crimson, toning into orange, brown and yellow, and ultimately into a very tender green framed amongst the darker green of the heather. The mere August visitor has no idea of the wonderful colouring which the blaeberry foliage imparts to the hills. When the sun shines upon the slopes of Caerketton the glow can be seen quite plainly from Comiston Road, a distance of about three miles; while from the road in the Logan glen the top of Carnethy is like the ruddy gold of ripe wheat. Amongst the cold gray rocks of Caerketton the blaeberries, now ruddy crimson and gold, now delicately yellow and green, run out and in, and up and down, in wavy wreaths and ribands. When seen under the spring sunshine—bright gleams intercepted now and again by towering masses of cumulus clouds, which cast broad shadows over square miles of land and sea—it seems to me that even the purple glow of August, the fullness of the summer, is equalled, I am tempted to say excelled, by the tender chastened beauty of this promise and prelude of summer amongst the hills. In September or October the same colour display is gone through, but in inverse order. The green changes to yellow, the yellow to brown, and the brown to orange, which finally bursts into a blaze of crimson and dies out as the autumn frosts begin to gather strength and sting. The long hill-slopes, when lighted by the rich colours of the blaeberries, glow like sunset skies.

The Beauty of the Blaeberry.

The graceful broom with its pendent flowers is almost a stranger to the hills, but the more aggressive, spiky whin asserts itself in many places. There is no season of the year when its rich yellow blossoms do not adorn the bare sunny banks on which it so often flourishes. On the slope between Swanston and Dreghorn there are various whin bushes, evidently of a great age and of a stunted growth, very thick and close, having no visible stems or branches, rounded in form—pruned by the keen north winds which sweep over them. They look like boulders on the hill-side. They have lost their green colour, and are almost as gray as the boulders. Quite as immovable, too, they are. The fiercest wind that blows causes no perceptible movement amongst them. I have stood on the tops of a few without their yielding in any way. In the moonlight or in the gray light of evening I have frequently mistaken them for boulders. The petty whin is also a native of the hills.

Wind-worn Whins and Trees.

In the hollow to the south of Allermuir and Caerketton, in which the tiny stream called Boghall Burn commences its short course, on the adjacent Fala Knowe, and in a few other situations, there are a number of juniper bushes—old, gnarled, twisted, lichen-covered, and most of them in the last stages of decay. They bring forth fruit, but it is as dry as dust in the mouth.

In the valleys, some of which are wonderfully sheltered, ornamental trees abound and flourish, but on the hills there are few, save Scots firs, spruces, and spindly larches, none of them of any great height, many of them decidedly dwarfish, dead

before their time, and stretching out scraggy
branches like bony arms and hands imploring the
mercy of the wintry heavens. In sheltered places
a few hazels grow, but their crop of nuts is of the
very scantiest. The hawthorn 'wi' its locks o' siller
grey' is to be 'pu'd' adjacent to—but not, I think,
on—the hills. The same may be said of the elder or
bourtree, and particularly of the rowan. Every one
who has been to any Highland ben intersected by
rocky glens cannot fail to have been struck by the
glorious colouring of the rowan foliage in September.
At a little distance it looks like a flaming fire—a fire
that always lights up on the northern side of the tree.
It is a great pity that there are not many more of
these lovely foliaged trees to lend an additional charm
to the beautiful glens and burns of the Pentlands.

Of ferns there is no great variety; few of the
rarer and finer kinds, so far as I have observed.
The little wall rue may be found in various places
amongst the rocks. The common polypody is
abundant in several situations. The hart's tongue
is a somewhat rare find; the maidenhair spleenwort
rarer still. The parsley fern I have seen
in one place, but, for obvious reasons, I do
not mention where. It is a pleasant surprise
to a tramper to meet with any of these rarer visitants
—something worthy of being noted in his diary. It
is like getting an unexpected introduction to a distinguished stranger. But, all the same, he recognises
that Nature is not dependent on these, her rarer and
delicate creations, for producing her most wonderful
effects. The male-fern, the lady-fern, the common
despised bracken in her hands are of far more

Ferns
and
Brackens.

decorative value in the mass than many others, with which for beauty and gracefulness of form they cannot compare singly. In summer, many of the hills are wreathed and festooned with the delicate green of these common yet beautiful ferns tossing in the wind. The Big Black Hill is very rich in ferns, and when the summer passes they produce many wonderful colour effects. If you want to see these, go in September when the purple of the heather still lingers in considerable quantity, and the early frosts have just touched the brackens, turning them here into yellow and there leaving them green—great simple masses of colour, with winding streaks of living green where the tiny spring-runs follow the devious courses of the little valleys. Or you may go later—in October—when the purple has faded from the heather, when later frosts have mellowed the ferns to a deep orange, and intensified by contrast the brilliant greens at the spring runs. It may be you will be favoured with a typical autumn day of calm and stately beauty; a circle of blue sky overhead, filmy clouds shading into silvery curtains draping the hills, golden sunshine over all, and purple haze softening and blending the ruddy colour of the screes, the orange of the brackens, and the green of the grass. When the fitful sunshine of the winter's day stretches a sudden finger and touches the hill-slopes the orange of the brackens is changed almost to glowing crimson.

A somewhat rare flowering plant, the cloud-berry —not found at a lower altitude than a thousand feet—grows in great abundance about the East and West Cairn Hills, and elsewhere in the neighbour-

hood. In late spring or early summer its leaves, of
a peculiarly vivid green, push up through the bents
and heather and unroll themselves somewhat after
the manner of the fronds of the adder's tongue fern,
while its white strawberry- or brambleberry- like
flowers in early June give the hill-top the appearance
of being thinly covered with snow. Later, when the
white, fairy-like petals drop off, they are succeeded
by the ruddy sepals, which expand quite like a
second flower, and are almost as beautiful as a flower.
Later still, generally in July, the orange or coral
coloured berries begin to form, when the sepals curl
over and clasp them. Amongst other places where I
have seen the cloud-berry in equal profusion I might
mention the top of the Cheviot. In that district
it is known as *noops*—said to be a corruption of
knop or knob, from the appearance of the fruit—and
noop jelly is esteemed a great delicacy in the north
of England. This plant is plentiful in Norway,
where it is known as ground mulberry, and is eaten
both raw and preserved. It is in truth a 'rare and
refreshing fruit.'

Occasional clumps of spiky, pale, evergreen crow-
berry, the fruit of which is known to some country
boys as *craw croops*, nestle amongst the darker green
of the heather.

On elevated marshy ground innumerable plants of
cotton-grass wave their little white flags in the wind,
Common and on dry knolls the thyme sheds its fine
Wild aromatic fragrance when the summer sun
Flowers. is hot. The bluebells of Scotland could
not be absent from the Pentlands ; neither, for shame,
could the thistles, both the purple and the white

flowered varieties—perhaps not the finest specimens, but certainly some of them very noble looking. During July and August some high-lying fields at Bavelaw are red with the flowering meadow sorrel, or *soorocks.*

The tall foxglove spire is a notable flower on many of the hill-sides. Why don't we spell the name of this magnificent flower properly? It should be folk's glove, meaning, of course, fairy's glove, not foxglove. Where I was brought up the flowers were called *wutches' thimmels* (witches' thimbles). John Burroughs, the American naturalist, thought the foxglove the most beautiful and conspicuous of all the wild-flowers he saw here, and adds that in America there is no conspicuous wild-flower to compare with it.

The purple scabious, or *curlie doddie,* is abundant in some places, with here and there a white variety—a freak which one meets with occasionally amongst most flowers.

Purple and yellow violets, or pansies, also the parti-coloured ones, the 'heartsease' of the old writers, dot many of the slopes; the yellow flowers glow like stars of gold amongst the rough bents. By the sides of the runnels and water-courses one will find the marsh marigold, with its glorious golden flowers; celandines in shady woods; and buttercups about the open, low-lying ground. Other yellow flowers one cannot fail to see are the fairy tormentils —like the yellow violets, golden stars amongst the green grass; and on exposed rocky places, where there is the thinnest covering of soil, the equally fairy-like rock rose. The tormentil is four-petalled,

cruciform; the rock rose is five-petalled. Both of
them are so fragile that they crumple up like
crushed tissue paper almost immediately on being
gathered. Other yellow flowers are the bird's foot
trefoil, which country children call *craw taes*, and
the woolly-looking lady's fingers, or kidney vetch.
Another is the ubiquitous dandelion, which the
imaginative Highlander calls 'the little flame of God.'
Its rich yellow flowers, not quite so rich as they are
to be met with under more favourable conditions
by the road-side hedges, but, all the same, 'leaping
at one like a smile, its homeliness pleasant as the
gladness of playing children.' An early yellow
flower is the coltsfoot. Its scientific name of
Tussilago Farfara has been corrupted into *tushilag*,
and under that name its dried withered leaves
used to be smoked by country boys—on the sly.

On the reservoir embankments, where the soil
is of the scantiest, and by the sides of some of the
paths, where it is only a little more plentiful, the
silver-weed maintains a stern fight with Nature,
spreads its glistening foliage over the wastes, and
displays its clear yellow flowers.

Lady's bedstraw, with its yellow flowers and its
honeyed scent, grows mostly about the roots of hedges;
but the white heath bedstraw covers large tracks of
the hills like 'the grymin' o' a new fa'n snaw.'
The hill shepherds call this plant *fog flooer*, that
is moss flower, and say that grass is always poor
where it flourishes. This seems to indicate that it is
a parasitic plant, feeding upon the roots of the
grasses, although the text-books do not say so.

The yellow rattle, with its abnormally inflated

calyx, is abundantly represented in many places. It is admittedly a parasitic plant.

The erect stem and brilliant yellow flower-heads of the golden-rod make it a conspicuous plant where it flourishes upon the hills. Equally conspicuous amongst the woods at Threipmuir is the ragweed or ragwort, a noble plant with its crown of yellow stars. It suffers, by comparison with other wild-flowers, from being too common. There are several varieties of the genus, *Senecio*, to which it belongs.

A remarkably pretty flower to be found in damp situations is the bog asphodel. Under the microscope it presents a charming appearance with its star-like shape and its stamens tipped with glowing orange.

Growing out of a chink in the garden wall at Dreghorn farmhouse there was once a good specimen of that handsome flower, the great mullein, but it failed to propagate itself.

A perfect garden of yellow flowers, including several varieties of hawkweed, hawkbit, hawksbeard, and cat's-ear, is to be found amongst the thick green grass at Harper Rig Reservoir. Groundsel and nipplewort dot the bare spots. The Water Trust representative is careful to protect the primroses in the glen at Glencorse Reservoir. A variety of St John's wort, with its fine graceful form, adorns the gravelly road bank at Loganlee Reservoir. Toad-flax is separated from the hills by merely the road's breadth near Hillend. Mimulus flowers abundantly in a little ditch, or burn, which is fed from the hills. Tansy I have gathered almost in touch with the heather. In at least two places comfrey grows in

some profusion, with its handsome foliage and its
rather colourless tubular flowers. At the boathouse
at Threipmuir there is a succession of flowers.
Spring is ushered in by snowdrops, followed by
primroses, and the fullness of summer is proclaimed
by the advent of honeysuckle and wild roses.

Of blue flowers the pretty veronica, or speedwell,
vulgarly known as *cat's een*, is sparingly distributed
about the lower slopes of some of the hills; forget-
me-not is plentiful in various wet places; and

Blooms
that
are Blue.

succory, with its pale lilac-blue flowers, is
an occasional find about the edges of bare
pasture-fields abutting on the hills. Most
of the forget-me-nots are long, spindly, ravelled-
looking plants, with miniature flowers. An exception
to this are, however, those which grow between

Threipmuir Cottage and Black Hill.

the joints of the stone pitching on the east embankment, where the road to Bavelaw crosses the top
of Threipmuir Reservoir. There they are dwarf,

three or four inches high, and the flowers, approaching to the size of daisies, are of a lovely colour. For at least half the year they are submerged by the waters of the reservoir. The finest forget-me-nots I have ever seen were growing upon the top of Ben Lawers, but these at Threipmuir are a good second. In the summer of 1916 the water in the reservoir was never low enough to permit of the flowering of the forget-me-nots.

The prettiest blue flower, in my opinion, found about the hills is the bugloss. It flourishes at the roots of an old hedge and round the edge of an old quarry near Hillend. Its flowers, in sheets like the blue of summer skies, lend a distinctive colouring to considerable areas, and can be seen from a distance. Nodding to the water, and almost dipping into it, the wild hyacinth, with its iron-blue flowers, was recently found by the side of one of the reservoirs. At a later date this flower was found growing in profusion on the lower northerly slope of the Big Black Hill.

Brooklime is somewhat restricted in its distribution. One place where I can recall having seen its beautiful blue flowers year after year is in the water-course which the path to the Green Cleuch crosses, just beyond the old quarry at Bavelaw. The devil's bit scabious grows abundantly in several situations, and I have found bugle flowering in at least one place on the hills.

In the shelter of woods, like a star of silver amongst the green grass, the white-petalled wood anemone, or wind-flower, dots the ground in early spring. Sometimes it will be found in exposed situations on the bare hills, during the roaring gales of March, tossing its head like a tiny bell. The wood sorrel, with its sensitive, little, purple-veined white flowers, and its trinity of leaves with their mystic symbolism, is also a gem to be found occasionally in the woodlands. It is considered by some writers to be the true shamrock. The water ranunculus, or crowfoot, blossoms when the reservoirs are low. It overgrows the water-courses too, White Petals. making them look as if they had been filled up with drifted snow. One must not forget the daisy, modest, hardy, perennial, flowering almost continuously.

In wet cleuchs and hopes the classical grass of Parnassus, with its single beautiful flower on each stalk, like a large white buttercup, is sparingly distributed. Another flower found in moist situations is angelica—one of the stately flowers, with its tall stem and spreading umbelliferous white top. Meadowsweet is also a frequenter of damp places. There is plenty of it round the margin of Threipmuir Reservoir, where its foamy cream-coloured flowers and feathery foliage adorn the water's edge and its perfume scents the air.

Hemlock, with its purple stem and mouse-like odour; sweet cicely, or myrrh, smelling of aniseed; coarse-leaved cow-parsnip, and feathery hedge parsley often crowd each other about the hedge roots by roads leading to the hills. The small flowers of mouse-ear are plentiful on the hills in places. Watercress abounds in various runnels—at the Rumbling Well, for instance. Winter-green, with its small bell-like flowers, I have not found on the Pentlands;

nor have I met with the pretty star-like flower
of the chickweed winter-green. I well remember
the wonderful impression the first sight of it made
upon me. A friend and I were climbing Monega
Hill, in Forfarshire, before sunrise on a July
morning, after having walked up Glenisla from
Alyth during the night. We were on our way to
Braemar. It was sultry and oppressive in the glen,
and the midges were ravenous. The cool air of the
mountain-side was very pleasant on our cheeks as we
climbed up amongst the dew-drenched grass, while
through the dim dawn shone the white stars of
chickweed winter-green.

Wood-sage, an inconspicuous white flower—dirty
white is its colour, as given in the text-books—grows
in great clumps on the hill-sides in the Logan
glen. It gives out a strong aromatic smell when
crushed.

A pretty wild-flower found growing in the same
situations as the grass of Parnassus is the lady's
smock. Its delicately pale lilac flowers are very
plentiful in various places. In certain parts of the
south of Scotland it is known under the poetical
name of *Jo Janet*.

Nestling close to the soil, the milkwort 'lifts its
modest head, the grassy tufts between.' Sometimes
it is in sufficient quantity to give its own distinctive
colouring—dark blue, light blue, pink, or white as
the case may be—to the hill-slope which it adorns.

The butterwort, an insectivorous plant, with its
purply blue flowers—somewhat like a violet—and its
sappy green leaves pressing close to the grass, is not
found in any great quantity ; but eyebright, sometimes

almost as short as the short grass, and occasionally
three or four inches in height, according to its situation, gives, like the milkwort, a note of colour to
considerable spaces of the hills.   It is believed to be
half parasitic on the roots of the grasses.

By the side of Threipmuir Reservoir, and in similar
situations, the sweet-smelling water-mint, with its
pale lilac flowers, can be gathered in great plenty.
Near the same place a numerous company of water-
avens stand in ranked rows, in their rusty-red
uniforms, like veterans of old wars.   Betony, with
its whorled spikes of purple flowers, darker
spotted, and its somewhat nettle-looking
leafage, is thinly scattered about the same
places; also hedge woundwort, with dull chocolate-
coloured flowers and even more pronounced nettle-
looking foliage, while the stately valerian lifts its
pale pink flowers above these humbler waterside
dwellers.

Pink, Red, and Purple.

At but two places on the hills have I made
acquaintance with the pink spire-like flower, and
the purple-blotched leaves of the spotted orchis.
The butterfly orchis, with its quaintly-shaped,
scented, cream-coloured flowers, was a late find
deserving of special mention.   I know of it in but
one place.   A beautiful and rare flower on the
Pentlands is the pale-purple, white-veined mountain
geranium.   I have found it in a small ravine amongst
the rocks at the Green Craigs, nestling at the foot
of a blackthorn bush.   Shaded from the sun and
sheltered from the blast, it was a most delicately
beautiful plant.   Like modest worth, it flourishes
sometimes in unlikely places.   Its dainty flowers

adorn the gloomy entrance to Hell's Hole. Herb-robert grows in similar situations.

A flower I was long in making acquaintance with on these hills is the stately rose-bay willow-herb. Its fine purply-pink or rose-coloured flowers and stems flourishing in a romantic situation add another to the many charms of the Pentlands. The same may be said of the meadow crane's-bill, with its handsome purply-blue flowers, and its equally handsome and richly-coloured autumn foliage.

The knapweeds, with their tough wiry stems and bright purple flowers, are hardy plants, and are fairly distributed over the hills; but the mallows are only occasionally met with. Self-heal—its botanical name of *Prunella Vulgaris* giving one the impression of something sham of shoddy, which its violet-purple flowers do not warrant — grows abundantly in moist grassy places; and fumitory, with its clusters of quaint rose-pink flowers and its dainty feathery foliage, is occasionally found as an escape from the potato-fields to the larger freedom of the hills. A pure white variety of self-heal was a little puzzling at first to place. I have seen but one specimen.

About the woods, particularly in the Loganlee glen, the red and white campion, and the meadow lychnis, or ragged robin, make a rich display of colour. Millefoil, or yarrow, of both the pink and white flowered varieties, is a common plant all over the hills. Bladder campion is sparingly distributed.

Pink-flowered knot-grass, like the poor, is ever present. It weaves its long trailing stems over the muddy bottoms of several of the reservoirs and

puts forth flowers when the retreating waters leave
these bare in the summer season.   Lady's mantle is
not nearly so plentiful on the Pentlands as it is on
many of the Highland mountains.   The democratic
stinging nettle often asserts itself in strange places,
indicating, they say, the presence of man, where
certainly one would never have expected man to
have dwelt.   The same may be said of the three
varieties of dead-nettle, red, white, and yellow,
although these are somewhat more aloof.   That
curious-looking plant, mare's tail, grows at the edge
of the water at Threipmuir.

It is not pretended that this is an exhaustive
list of the flowers found on the hills.   There may
be others, but I can vouch that at one time or
another I have seen every one of those mentioned,
and derived pleasure from the sight of them all.

'The Range' from Nine Mile Burn Path.

EPILOGUE.

ALL walkers are of opinion that there is no recreation to compare with walking, and all hill-walkers are convinced that in hill-walking is to be found the highest form of this noble art.

Since the advent of so many of those things which a distinguished Edinburgh editor has graphically called 'stink stoories,' road-walking is out of the question. On the roads the walker is crowded into the ditch or up the bank; in summer he is The Compleat Walker. suffocated with dust, and in winter he is splashed with mud. Under such conditions there is neither pleasure nor profit in road-walking. The only refuge for the walker is amongst the hills. One of our proverbs speaks of making a virtue of necessity. The hill-walker is only too pleased at the necessity which has driven him to the hills, and seeks not to justify his going there on any ground of making a virtue thereof.

Without question hill-walking is the most delightful exercise in which anyone can indulge. It has so many things to recommend it. It is steady, sustained, not too violent, brimful of interest. It can be pursued at all seasons. It conduces to calmness and evenness of mind. It keeps the pores open, the pulse strong, the nerves steady, the liver active, the digestion good. It leads to plain living and high thinking, and is a safe antidote to the modern vulgar craving after unnatural excitement. On the hill-side a crust of bread and a draught of spring water are far more to the walker than a feast of fat things. A friend of the writer's, a brother tramp, speaks of his Pentland walking— and especially of the rushes down the steep slopes and screes, for which he is famous—as ' Pentland pills for liver ills.' Hill-walking is the shortest and the surest way to the attainment of the ideal condition of having a sound mind in a sound body. More than early rising it will make one healthy and wise, and it will not fail to make one wealthy too, with the best of all possible wealth—a mind well stored with the facts of nature, and a heart filled with a deep and wide sympathy embracing in its range every living thing.

Think, too, of the numerous other studies and exercises which can be conjoined with hill-walking, such as geology, botany, natural history, angling, sketching, weather lore, and so forth. Last, but not least, as an amusement and exercise hill-walking is cheap. It costs next to nothing. Perhaps in this lies its reproach. We are not simple enough in our tastes to become walkers. Walking is too slow and too cheap. The craze for mere speed is overwhelming us. We flee over the earth, and we fly through the air. We crave for the unnatural, for excitement, for the grand, for the theatrical. Too often we cross continents and seas, and know not that what we seek lies at our very doors. We prefer the crowds, the reek and the foul air of the theatre, the music-hall and the tavern, to the sweetness and the beauty, the grandeur, the exhilaration, and the calm restful repose of nature which are to be found on the hill-top. How true it is, as Emerson